Toddler sense

TODDLER SENSE

Understanding your toddler's sensory world – the key to a happy, well-balanced child

Ann Richardson

Dedicated to Ellen and Maeve

Published by Metz Press
1 Cameronians Avenue
Welgemoed, 7530
South Africa

First published in 2005
Second impression, January 2006
Third impression, September 2006

PUBLISHER AND EDITOR	Wilsia Metz
CONSULTANT	Kerry Wallace (Occupational Therapist)
DESIGN AND LAY-OUT	Alinda Metz
COVER PHOTOGRAPH	Rikki van Zyl, Organic Design Studio
ILLUSTRATIONS	Annette van Zyl
PRODUCTION	Andrew de Kock
REPRODUCTION	Cape Imaging Bureau, Cape Town
PRINTING AND BINDING	Paarl Print, 22 Oosterland Street, Dal Josafat
ISBN 10	1-919992-17-0
ISBN 13	978-1-919992-17-4

Consultant Kerry Wallace qualified as an Occupational Therapist from UCT in 1979. She has been working in paediatric private practice in Johannesburg for the past 16 years. Sensory Integration is her passion and she trains young therapists in this field and in the assessment and treatment of babies, toddlers, and pre-schoolers with Sensory Integration Disorder. Another special interest is early intervention in children with Autistic Spectrum Disorders. She qualified in Neurodevelopmental Therapy in the USA.

AUTHOR'S ACKNOWLEDGEMENTS

The feeling of personal gratification after I finished writing my first book ***Baby sense*** (co-authored with Megan Faure) in 2002 was unsurpassed. Knowing that ***Baby sense*** has been there for so many desperate parents, I knew that it was time for a toddler version to 'grow up' with all the precious ***Baby sense*** babies out there.

Toddler sense is a combination of many years' worth of both personal and professional lessons and experiences that life has brought my way. Being a mother to my two daughters, Ellen and Maeve, has taught me the best lessons about parenting and patience, but most of all about unconditional love.

To my friend and esteemed colleague Kerry Wallace (Occupational Therapist), thank you for your help with this project – your most valuable contribution and input. I know it was a labour of love for you, and I will never forget that. Megan, even though we haven't worked together on this book, thank you for all your support and encouragement – there would be no ***Toddler sense*** without ***Baby sense,*** and I will always remember you as a significant part of my life!

I will always be grateful to all my extended family, friends and colleagues for their enthusiasm and encouragement while writing ***Toddler sense*** and I especially thank Jayne Eurelle for her professional advice, and two very special nursing colleagues, Debbie Hooper and Sue Wohlfarth for their continual support and for keeping the practice going – I would never have managed without you!

Grateful thanks go to the publishing team at Metz Press, particularly to Wilsia Metz for believing in me a second time, and for all her support, love and wisdom.

Deep gratitude and a very special place in my heart is reserved for all those wonderful families I have had the honour of dealing with professionally over the last twenty odd years. Thank you for sharing your babies with me – you continue to provide me with inspiration.

Special thanks to Professor André Venter who, despite his incredibly busy schedule, took the time to read *Toddler sense* and write such an insightful foreword.

To my beloved parents – even though you're somewhere else now, I still feel you near me – thank you for your love and encouragement and for making me who I am today.

I don't even know where to start to thank my special husband Ken – nothing would be possible for me without his unfailing love and support – thank you for always being there for me and for loving me the way you do.

Finally, all credit, love and thanks, always, to our Heavenly Father, the Creator of all.

Contents

FOREWORD

Your baby has had his or her first birthday. Congratulations! But just when you thought that your concerns as a parent were going to diminish, you are suddenly confronted with a whole new deck of developmental issues!

After the success of her first book, ***Baby sense*** (co-authored with Megan Faure), Ann Richardson has now produced a very useful guide to address the development of toddlers.

In our modern society 'stimulation' of our children has become quite a buzz word. Yet, with a common sense approach and a general awareness of when things go wrong, parents are usually quite able to provide for all the needs of their children. Knowledge is power!

In her book ***Toddler sense***, Richardson not only provides useful algorithms to monitor all aspects of your child's development, she also has a "no mess, no fuss" approach to solving some of the common problems in this age group, such as sleep disorders.

I am sure this book will be a useful source for all parents (and grandparents!) With its easy chatty style, it is not only easily understood, but entertaining. The reference to real-case scenarios, allows parents to understand that their problems or concerns may not be unique.

So settle back and enjoy the amazing and amusing world of your toddler!

Prof André Venter
Developmental Paediatrician
Academic Head: Department of Paediatrics and Child Health
University of the Free State

National Chairman: Paediatric Neurology and Developmental Association of Southern Africa (PANDA-SA)

Introduction

Congratulations! You have reached the magical milestone of having survived the first year of parenthood. The days and seemingly endless nights with a fussy newborn are, thankfully, now a distant memory, as are the heady days of each and every new baby milestone reached. Parenting has taken on a new role. You are now feeling like an 'old hat' at this game, and dispense freely of your advice around the dinner table to friends who have just become parents. Suddenly push carts, dinky little shoes with laces and kiddies cutlery sets seem much more interesting than rattles and mobiles.

The toddler years are the transition between the baby your child has outgrown and the child he is becoming. Let him enjoy them, savour them and let him exhilarate in all the new feelings and experiences he will encounter as his world opens up beyond just you, his parents or caregivers.

During the toddler years, his body and mind will develop in leaps and bounds. However, the downside is that he is generally able to focus only on *his own* needs and desires (much like teenagers!) He will start to develop a will of his own, and will be able to only see things from *his* point of view. While his memory and imagination are developing, his thinking is non-logical and non-reversible.

Most toddlers live for the moment, have more power than sense and will be inclined to rush headlong into all sorts of behaviours with absolutely no regard for any danger, self control or consequences! Your toddler will spot what he wants, and set off to get it, unaware of the crocodile pit on the way!

His language skills are developing, so he is more able to communicate. Interaction with other children in the early years of toddlerhood is pretty limited to pushing, poking and shoving. Don't lose heart though; he will start to show an interest in other children, and by about the age of 3 years, will have learnt how to play with, as opposed to alongside, his peers, share toys and games and develop friendships.

Toddlerhood is a time of tantrums, teething, and conflict, but it is also a time of tremendous growth and development, both physically and emotionally. Soon it will be time to wave goodbye to your child at the pre-school gate, and you will wonder where the toddler years went. You may ask yourself, "Was it really 3 years ago that he took his first wobbly steps? Has he really been having conversations with me for the past 2 years? Perhaps I can un-child proof my home now ..."

It is very important that parents understand what constitutes normal toddler behaviour. If you have an understanding of what to expect from a toddler and accept and respect that that behaviour is quite normal for the space where your child is at *right now*, it will go a long way towards effective, guilt-free and realistic parenting

Dr Christopher Green in his book *Toddler Taming Tips* (Vermillion, 2003) says that this period of time in your child's life is characterised by certain goals for toddlers and specific roles for parents.
Your role as a parent is to
- guide gently;
- set limits and introduce controls;
- avoid confrontation; and
- be 100 per cent firm when needed.

Your toddler's goals are to
- learn to control his body and behaviours;
- be able to separate from his parents;
- learn that tantrums don't always work;
- become toilet trained; and
- learn to share possessions and respect others' rights and possessions.

Imagine that your child is faced with a huge, empty canvas. As he grows and develops from a one-year-old tottering around on chubby legs, to a round toddler with a big head, to the more athletic build of the pre-schooler, he will 'paint' his way through these exciting and wondrous years, taking you with him on this precious journey. Join me as I accompany you on this journey, helping you to understand your child better so that you can help him benefit best from his world.

I would suggest that you read the book from start to finish first as many different issues are discussed in each chapter. The first part of the book will explain to you how your toddler's brain works, and how important his sensory and perceptual development is to his overall development. It also covers issues such as reading his signals, understanding and dealing with sleeping, toilet training, behaviour and discipline issues. The second half of the book discusses general care and development in age-related sections with specific regard to issues such as nutrition, routines, stimulation, behaviour and sleep. This will give you a clear understanding of your toddler from the word go.

Toddlerhood ends at the age of four, as it is at this age that your child enters the world of the pre-schooler where life becomes a bit more serious and structured. So enjoy these heady and exciting years – they pass by all too quickly.
I found this lovely poem by a mom, Nalani Madurai, in the *Your Baby* magazine (November 2004) and I think that it sums up exactly what a toddler is. Keep this and read it when the going gets tough – it is bound to bring a smile to your face. Not having any contact details for Nalani, I would like to thank her here for her words of wisdom.

If it is on, I must turn it off

If it is off, I must turn it on

If it is folded, I must unfold it

If it is a liquid, it must be shaken, then spilled

If it is a solid, it must be crumbled, chewed or smeared

If it is high, it must be reached

If it is shelved, it must be unshelved

It if is pointed, it must be run with at top speed

If it is plugged, it must be unplugged

If it is in the trash, it must be removed, inspected, and thrown on the floor

If it is closed, it must be opened

If it is full, it will be more interesting emptied

If it is a stroller, it must under no circumstances be ridden in without protest, it must be pushed by me instead

If it has a flat surface, it must be banged upon

If mommy's hands are full, I must be carried

If mommy is in a hurry and wants to carry me, I must walk alone

If it is paper, it must be torn

If it has buttons, they must be pressed

If the volume is low, it must go high

If it is a drawer, it must be pulled upon

If it is a bug, it must be swallowed

If it doesn't stay on my spoon it must be dropped on the floor

If it is not food, it must be tasted

If it is dry, it must be made wet with drool, milk or toilet water

If it is a car seat, I must protest

If it is Mommy, it must be hugged

I AM A TODDLER – watch me grow!

Understanding the brain and the sensory system

CHAPTER 1

Now that Melissa has become mobile, her world has taken on a whole new meaning! She can now stand on her own two feet all by herself, and has just managed to take a few steps forward. She is even managing to get back onto her bottom and up again all on her own. It feels really strange to see the world from this position – everything looks so different, even Mom and Dad! Needless to say, Melissa's parents can't believe their precious daughter is now so grown up! It seems like just the other day that she was a helpless little newborn.

Your toddler begins to learn through her senses from the day she is born. In fact, her senses start developing shortly after conception. Her sensory system is the very special part of her nervous system that receives and processes information in the brain. It is through this process that her brain will grow and develop. Her brain is constantly growing and changing and also, importantly, develops an amazing ability to organise itself. If you would like to read more about sensory development in the womb, *Baby sense* (Megan Faure & Ann Richardson, Metz Press, 2002) has a chapter dedicated to this subject.

THE KEY TO KNOWLEDGE

Melissa's sensory system unlocks the door to her learning and knowledge, because how she learns, feels and thinks is dependent on her sensory system, through which all her experiences of the world are processed. Isn't it amazing to think that her memory base patterns are forming and developing as she grows and experiences her sensory world.

AN AMAZING THOUGHT

> How your child interprets sensory information shapes her experience of her world, whilst at the same time, her sensory system is shaped by her experiences of the world.

As you are reading these words, your brain is constantly monitoring the sounds, smells, temperature and light around you. It knows which muscles are tense, which are relaxed and where they all are. Your brain is monitoring all the functions of your body's organs, as well as every touch and pressure on your body, whilst at the same time making constant muscle adjustments to keep your eyes and your body aligned to the book in front of you. It enables you to read the words on the page, then integrate and understand each word and meaning, in its context, so that you can benefit from the experience. Isn't that simply amazing?

THE BRAIN

The brain is made up of millions of nerves. Most of us are born with a full complement of nerve cells (neurons). These neurons are specialised cells designed to transmit electrical messages throughout the body. This process of nerve cells connecting and networking is the very basis of learning and thought. When your baby was a newborn, her brain was very immature and she was very limited as to what she could do. As she started to grow, develop and learn from her world, the cells of her nervous system (neurons) began to connect in complex patterns forming neural pathways. These neural pathways are constantly being organised and reorganised throughout her life, allowing her to grow and develop.

The main function of our brain is to be in continuous communication with the rest of our body. Most importantly, the brain receives information from the environment (via our sensory system), and then decides whether this incoming information is important or relevant. The brain then has to interpret that information so that an appropriate response can occur. For example, removing our hand from a hot surface. This can be illustrated as follows (diagram from *Baby sense*):

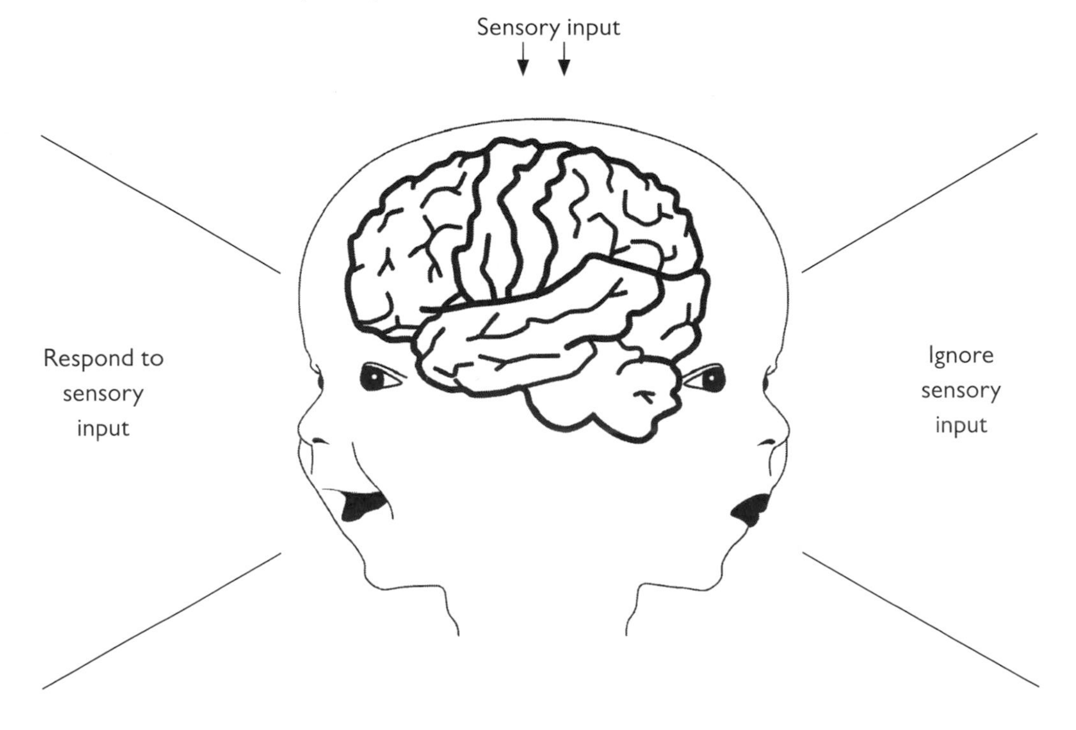

THE SENSORY SYSTEM

The sensory neurons (or nerve cells) deliver sensory information from the body to the spinal cord and brain (central nervous system). Did you know that there are five times more nerves in the brain to receive and organize this sensory information than there are nerves responsible for movement? Melissa's sensory experiences are delivered to her body externally via her ***exteroceptors*** – her ***skin*** (touch), her ***tongue*** (taste), her ***ears*** (hearing), her ***eyes*** (visual) and her ***nose*** (smell). Her ***proprioceptors*** give her information internally about her world. These sensors are found inside tendons, muscles and joints, telling her about her body position and how her limbs are moving. The ***vestibular*** sense – her sense of movement – is part of this. This sense organ is located in the mechanism of her inner ear. Melissa also receives information from all the organs of her body. These sensors are called ***interoceptors*** and they give her information such as the feeling that her tummy is full.

Let's go on a 'journey of the senses' to see how your toddler is interpreting her world via her sensory system.

Touch

Touch is an integral, natural part of life. Our skin contains touch receptors which give us information about pain, pressure (deep and light), temperature and also tells us what our bodies are up to (via our muscles, tendons and movement). The sense of touch is vital to our emotional well-being. Touch is a strong anchor in behaviour and learning, so much so, that the absence of touch may slow down nerve development and lead to developmental delay. Touch also plays an important role in our appreciation of new experiences, for example once Melissa can talk, she will always say, "Let me see that" whilst reaching out to touch an object.

Sight

Melissa's eyes are the trusted windows to her world. Her eyes register light, colour and objects (form). When her sense of sight matured at around eight months, she became capable of seeing from near to far, as well as to perceive dimension and depth. Her eyes are in constant motion gathering sensory information to build up images and memories which are necessary for learning. When she stops moving her eyes, they no longer take in any new sensory information. The only processing happening then is actually inside her brain. This is why, when Melissa fixates and stares at something hard, she may be unaware of her environment!

Smell

Receptors in the nose pick up smells in the environment. Billions of tiny hair cells inside the bridge of the nose (which is situated in the frontal lobe of the brain) stimulate nerves in the brain to perceive any smells in the environment. Sensations from the nose are the only ones that go directly to the emotional centre of our brain. That is why smell is so strongly linked to memory and why it plays such an important role in emotional regulation. Think of a situation when a smell in the air immediately brings back a flood of memories such as the antiseptic smell of a doctor's surgery. Smell is also used to alert us to danger. Pheromones (a type of hormone) are released when one is afraid. These have a scent which can be picked up by animals and children.

Taste

The sense of taste is closely linked to smell. Melissa's senses of smell and taste have been functional from 28 weeks of gestation when she was still in the womb. Taste buds are found all over the tongue, and their purpose is to register the taste of any substance that comes into contact with the tongue. Different receptors are sensitive to sweet, sour, bitter and salty tastes.

Hearing

We know that by 28 weeks of gestation Melissa's sense of hearing was fully developed. Since it is one of her earliest senses to develop, hearing is very important for Melissa as it alerts her brain to incoming stimuli, whether for protection or understanding. By Melissa identifying where the sound comes from and then attaching a meaning to each sound, the learning process is stimulated. Sound is carried on airwaves picked up by receptors found in the ear, and registered in the brain. Martie Pieterse in her book *School readiness through play* (Metz press, 2001) says that a child who is able to hear and listen well learns faster, makes fewer mistakes, and is less easily frustrated.

Movement (vestibular sense)

This is the first sensory system to develop fully in the womb (by twenty weeks of gestation). This sense controls our sense of movement and balance. Receptors in the inner ear sense changes in our position in space, more specifically, movement of our head in space. When this sense is working well, we know in which direction we are moving, how fast we are going, and whether we are speeding up or slowing down. When it functions optimally, we don't become nauseous or feel threatened by normal movement. The connection between the vestibular system and the brain is crucial. Melissa needs to move to activate and stimulate this system, to enable her to take in information from her environment, which is necessary to stimulate her brain. Effective processing of the vestibular system is vital for the development of the stomach and back muscles. These muscles are the backbone of all motor (movement) activity. Activation of the vestibular system enables a baby to move from primitive patterns at birth, to sitting, crawling, standing, and walking by challenging the sense of gravity during her first year. From this basic sense of understanding gravity, Melissa will develop balance as she grows (such as learning to walk on a plank).

Body position (proprioception)

Proprioception is the sense of body position and equilibrium. It is often referred to as 'the hidden sense'. Proprioceptors are found in all our muscles, joints, tendons and in the inner ear (vestibular). They are sense organs that relay information from our joints and muscles – whether they are tense or relaxed, and whether they are busy or still – to give the body a sense of itself in space.

It is important for Melissa's body to know what position she is in and how her limbs are moving. Proprioceptors give Melissa's brain feedback to maintain optimal muscle contraction and relaxation. Simply put, proprioceptors are Melissa's learning tools as she explores her world with her body.

Most importantly though, is the role that her proprioceptors play in calming and regulating her emotions. For example a hug from Mom works like magic for a distressed toddler.

Interoception

This comes from sensors in Melissa's internal organs relaying information to her brain about her needs and comfort levels. These sensations include hunger, digestion, body temperature and elimination. For example, her digestive system will send a message that it is time for a meal.

HABITUATION

Our entire body is designed as a finely tuned sensory receptor for gathering information from our environment. As adults we can, to a large extent, control what sensory information we take in by simply controlling our environment to the best of our ability. However, before we are even conscious of any sensory information we may have received, our brain will determine whether this information is important to us or not. If it is not important, the brain has the ability to filter out or inhibit this information by recognising that it is familiar input and then deciding to no longer focus on it. This process is called **habituation**. An example of habituation is that we do not always feel the label of our clothing resting against our skin – this input has been ***habituated*** so that it doesn't reach our consciousness.

Focus

Habituation is crucial as it allows us to focus on important information without becoming over-stimulated. So, as you sit reading this, you are able to focus on the words in front of you, and not be distracted by the smell of cooking from the kitchen, or the sound of your toddler banging on her toy drum!

Parents or care-givers of toddlers develop the most amazing habituation skills, and can shut out the cacophony of noise that toddlers seem to make. However, our finely tuned antennae soon pick up the sound of anything seriously amiss! In your toddler's case however, if this process of habituation is impaired, too much unimportant stimulation will flood her nervous system leading to sensory overload, or over-stimulation.

Regulate

In the first year of life, your baby's ability to habituate was underdeveloped. This is why you had to regulate how much stimulation your child was exposed to. You also had to filter out and monitor certain sensory input into her nervous system. Now that your baby is a year old, she should be able to habituate the feel of her clothing on her skin, certain sounds and smells in her environment, as well as movement.

Anything new and novel in your toddler's environment will cause her to be alert and interested – this is how she will constantly learn. If the stimulus is familiar, she will habituate it quickly, and will be able to ignore that stimulus in her environment. For example, Melissa may appear disinterested in the basket containing her familiar toys, but will show great interest in a visiting friend's red fire engine. In order for Melissa to develop her habituation skills, she needs to be exposed to a variety of different stimuli on a regular basis, including

- All movement activities;
- Lots of touch (tactile) exploration;
- Exposure to a variety of food textures and tastes, so that she can experience biting, chewing, sucking, blowing and swallowing.

See table on the effect of stimulation on state, pages 28–30.

Self-regulation

As Melissa develops from an infant to a round toddler with a big head, to the more athletic build of the pre-schooler, the role that Melissa's parents play in *maintaining* her in an optimal state of being either alert or calm, begins to diminish as Melissa is able to **take control by self-regulation**. However, it is still important to regulate the type of sensory input she receives, as well as to filter out excessive sensory input by avoiding over-stimulation to prevent sensory overload. See pages 28–30 for suggestions to help her take control by self-regulation.

Habituation is essential for the development of concentration. You already know that when your baby was seven months old, she easily got bored with stimuli to which she was repeatedly exposed. In order to stimulate Melissa effectively, her mom needs to remain one step ahead of her ability to habituate! So she will need to rotate her toys frequently, expose her to a world outside of her home, and keep her active!

Some children register every stimulus in their environment, battle to habituate and therefore cannot stay focused on one activity for long (much like you feel when your toddler keeps on interrupting you during a task!). Other toddlers may need a lot more intensive stimuli or input to interest them in an activity in the first place and to sustain that level of interest.

So you can see how important it is to understand how your toddler's sensory system works. This will help you to know when, why and how to nurture, stimulate or calm her. It will also help you to enhance her physical and mental development with appropriate stimulation, while at the same time keeping her happy, calm and content. Age-appropriate stimulation is discussed in more detail in separate age-specific chapters in the second half of the book.

SENSE-ABLE SECRET

What *your toddler knows,* **what** *she feels,* **what** *she thinks and* **what** *she learns, is moulded by* **how** *she knows,* **how** *she feels,* **how** *she thinks and* **how** *she learns. In other words, all of what she experiences as she goes through life, will help to develop her brain.*

There is so much in the world for us all
If we only have the eyes to see it,
And the heart to love it,
And the hand to gather it to ourselves.

Lucy Maud Montgomery

Perceptual development

CHAPTER 2

Nicholas is now 2 years old. His mom finds it hard to believe that only a year ago, he was still very wobbly on his feet, and was only able to carry out simple tasks. Now, as she fondly watches him playing with his tipper truck on the floor, she realizes what a long way he has come. How is it that he 'knows' that when he spins the wheels of his truck (motor planning) they make a certain noise (auditory association), and that the back section of the truck tips over (visual association)? His sensory system is constantly enabling him to learn from his environment so that he is now able to play with purpose and explore, as opposed to the automatic reflexive behaviour he showed when he was younger. A major part of this amazing learning curve is the development of Nicholas' ability to process, and generalise the information he receives from his sensory systems (perceptual development).

Perceptual development is the process whereby Nicholas is able to recognise, organise (or combine), interpret and classify all the information that his sensory system is gathering as he goes about his daily activities. This registration of sensory input is the very first vital step, and obviously Nicholas' sensory system must be functional in order for this to occur. Unless Nicholas is able to concentrate on playing with his truck and remember what he is doing with it, he cannot make sense (perceive) what is happening in his world. Most of this contact with his world will occur through seeing and hearing. Perception is the meaning that his brain **gives** to the messages that are received via his sensory system. In other words, Nicholas will **see** the truck, and his brain will tell him that it is his truck (visual perception). He will **hear** the noise of the wheels, and his brain will tell him that the noise is coming from the truck's wheels (auditory perception) – so he will learn to associate a certain sound with the wheels of the truck. He will also be aware of where his body ends and where the truck begins (spatial perception).

Visual, auditory and spatial perception are all absolutely essential abilities your child needs to master in order for him to understand and learn from his environment. For ideas on how to enhance visual, auditory and spatial perception, please refer to the age-specific chapters in the second half of the book. To see how it works, let's look at each area of perception in a bit more detail.

VISUAL PERCEPTION

It is important that Nicholas is able to give meaning to what his eyes see. He needs to be able to identify, interpret, and categorise ***what*** he sees in a correct manner. He then needs to compare this information with the memory of previous sensory experiences (what he has seen, heard, touched or felt in past experience). This process is called **visual perception**, which is the process whereby he can identify, organise and interpret visual stimuli. This will eventually enable him to recognise and use different symbols, to learn to read and write and to learn mathematical skills. There are four different aspects of visual perception that you need to be aware of as you watch your toddler grow up and become a pre-schooler:

Shape perception

This is his ability to recognise an object as the same regardless of its position, size, background or texture. For example, Nicholas will be able to recognise a block even if it is made of velvet instead of plastic; he will realize that a drawing of a dog is the same as a real live dog. He will also realize that if an object is either far or near, it may look like it has a different shape, but it is actually the same thing.

Visual discrimination

This is his ability to spot the differences and similarities between objects very quickly by perceiving the finer details. This will enable him to put all the lego in one container and the cars in another.

Visual analysis

This is his ability to see a recognisable object (that he has *previously* learnt about, using his long term memory), both as a whole and as different pieces that can be put together again. For example, even if Nicholas can only see the wheels of his truck, he knows that this is the truck that he is looking for.

Visual figure-ground perception

This is his ability to focus on one object in a busy background, for example finding the red car in a toy-box filled with many colourful objects. When Nicholas is in a group setting he will be able to concentrate on climbing the bottom rung of the jungle gym, even if there are other children alongside him. This is an important building block for the development of concentration.

SPATIAL PERCEPTION

Spatial perception is a toddler's ability to observe the position of objects in relation to himself, and in relation to each other. Nicholas has to know how much space he needs to move in, otherwise he would be constantly bumping into objects or other children and knocking them over. Learning to *use* his body effectively in space enables him to explore, and move into unknown space with confidence. This will provide him with many more opportunities to explore his world. As your toddler grows into his pre-school years, spatial perception is important for him so that he can understand that there is a back and a front, an upside and a downside, an inside and an outside.

Another important skill that develops out of spatial perception is **sequencing**. This is your child's ability to organise and comprehend the steps (or sequence) in a process or event. Nicholas knows that his socks go on before his shoes. Sequencing is vital for language and reading skills and for understanding the order of events in life.

AUDITORY PERCEPTION

Auditory perception is the ability that your toddler develops to attach *meaning* to all the sounds that he hears. This is a very important aspect of his language development. As we know, language development is crucial for his intellectual development. As your toddler grows up and becomes a pre-schooler, there are three important aspects of auditory perception you need to be aware of.

Auditory discrimination

This is your child's ability to distinguish between various sounds – some may sound similar, and some different. It also helps him to pick up the difference in intensity of sound (is it loud or soft?), duration (is it short or long?), pitch (is it high or low?), and at what intervals he hears it (is it regular or irregular?).

Auditory analysis

Your toddler needs to be able to do auditory analysis to break up the sounds of a word, and to also form a word by combining (or synthesizing) these sounds.

Auditory foreground-background perception

This is his ability to hone in and focus on a specific sound, even if there are other sounds around in the background – for example Nicholas will hear and respond to his mother calling him when engrossed in his favourite game. This is also an important foundation for concentration.

THE IMPORTANCE OF MEMORY

Memory is when input is interpreted (via the sensory system) and then stored in the brain so that it can be retrieved when necessary. Memory is usually rich with sensations of sight, sound, smell, taste, emotions and movement. The development of your toddler's auditory memory, for example, is closely linked to his future spelling and reading ability. There are different types of memory.

Short-term memory

This refers to the retention of information over a period of seconds or minutes. Only a small amount of material can be stored in the short-term memory and it is quickly forgotten. For example, Nicholas may have put a small object into the back of his truck when he played with it two days ago. He would have looked for it in the right place if you had asked him about it right then. However, he has forgotten about this object by now, and does not look for it when he takes his truck out now.

Long-term memory

This is the storage of learnt material over hours, days or years. The more emotionally charged an experience, the better it will be remembered, for example a visit to Granny or to the circus. Large amounts of information can be stored in the long-term memory, and sensory experiences associated with the event will help to trigger the memory, for example smells, tastes, sounds.

Recall

This is when the input and response is remembered in its original form. Recall is the ability to reproduce the original input accurately on demand, in the absence of the original stimulus. Nicholas will remember that his truck is blue and will recognise it.

Recognition

This is the remembering of a stimulus and being able to identify it accurately on re-presentation. When Nicholas looks at a photograph of himself playing with his truck, he will recognise it as being his.

Kinaesthetic memory

This is the memory for movement patterns, such as learning to ride a tricycle, or to brush your teeth.

MEMORY SKILLS

Without memory skills, a lot of information needed for learning new concepts will be lost, and the learning process will not occur.

Take time to be friendly – it is the road to happiness.
Take time to dream – it is hitching your wagon to a star.
Take time to love and to be loved – it is the privilege of the Gods.
Take time to look around – it is too short a day to be selfish.
Take time to laugh – it is the music of the soul.

Old English saying

CHAPTER 3

The effect of sensory input on your toddler's state

Delia is a typical, busy two-year-old. Her endless energy and eagerness to learn amaze her parents who do their best to keep her stimulated and happy. When Delia is awake and happy, she responds with pleasure to this stimulation, becoming more attentive and alert as her nervous system is flooded with input. However, as time goes by and she becomes overloaded by this input, she reacts by becoming irritable and weepy. If Delia is lucky, her mom will know when to be calm and gentle with her and will remove excessive stimulation from Delia's environment to help her shut down and prepare for some quiet or sleep time.

To have a better understanding of the effect of sensory input or stimulation on your toddler, it is important to look at the states her brain moves through in a day. In a 24 hour day, your child will spend part of it awake, and part of it asleep. These 2 states are clearly different, but what is important to know is that within each of these two states, there are other identifiable states.

SLEEP STATES

There are two states of sleep – **light sleep** (or rapid eye movement sleep) and **deep sleep** (or non-rapid eye movement sleep). Light sleep is usually characterized by fluttering eyelids and restlessness, and it is from this light sleep that most children stir easily. Deep sleep is when your child sleeps so soundly that she barely appears to be breathing.

WAKEFUL STATES

Your toddler also has many wakeful states. The state just before she goes to sleep and just after she wakes up is called the **drowsy** state. This is when she may have heavy or droopy eyes, and will often stare into space, not focusing on much at all. As she continues to wake up, she will become responsive, but will remain calm and content. This is the **calm-alert** state. She is focused, enjoys interaction and is attentive. When she is in this state, she will learn and benefit the most from her environment. However, if she becomes over-stimulated at this stage, she will then enter the **active-alert** state where she will become fidgety and active. When she is in this state, she won't be in the best state for learning as her brain is receiving too much input from her muscles which are busy moving. This movement stimulation may distract her brain from learning anything from her world at that time. In this active-alert state she also runs the risk of sensory overload. It won't be long before she will be irritable and may move into the **crying** state.

SENSE-ABLE SECRET
Use alerting or stimulatory sensory input when your toddler is in the ***calm-alert state.*** *This is the best state for learning.*

HOW SENSORY INPUT AFFECTS THESE STATES

Visualize these different states in ascending order, with crying at the top, and deep sleep at the bottom. Let's see how sensory input affects the states:

Stimulating, **distressing** or **alerting input** will most likely move your child **up** a state. So, a loud noise (stimulatory) can move her from a state of deep sleep into light sleep, or may in fact even wake her up. Gentle stimulation such as softly playing music may ease her from the drowsy state into the calm-alert state, but if it is played too loudly, she may go from calm-alert through active-alert and straight into the crying state.

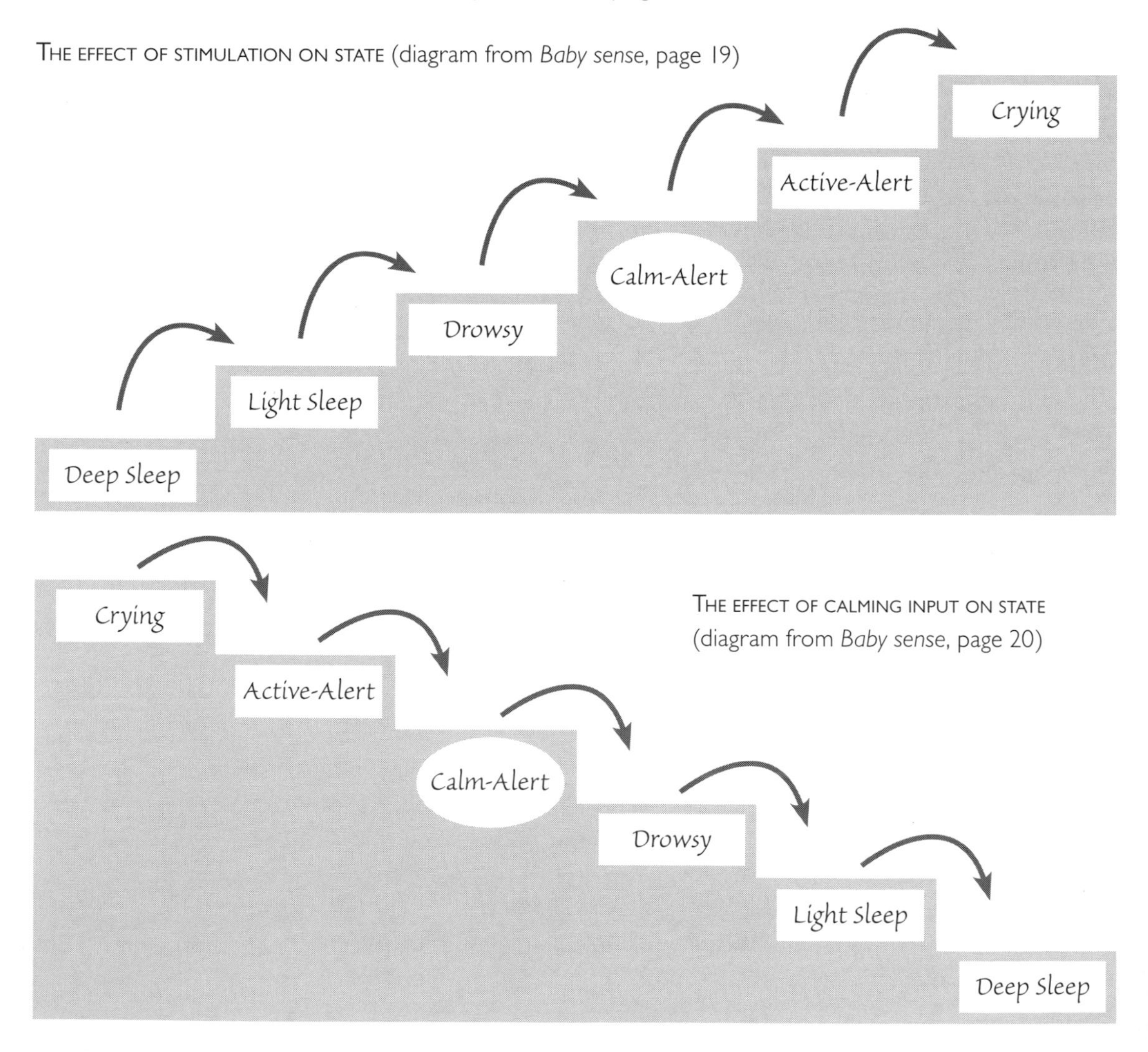

THE EFFECT OF STIMULATION ON STATE (diagram from *Baby sense*, page 19)

THE EFFECT OF CALMING INPUT ON STATE (diagram from *Baby sense*, page 20)

Calming input, on the other hand, is inclined to move your toddler's state **down** a level. If her nervous system is calmed with calming input, her state calms down too. Gentle touch may help move her from a drowsy state into a light sleep state. Rocking her gently may soothe her when she is in a crying state, helping to calm her, and may even make her drowsy.

REGULATING YOUR TODDLER'S STATE

Each toddler has a unique threshold for different types of stimulation. This simply means that while one toddler can remain in the calm-alert state for some time, even in a very busy environment, another one becomes over-stimulated very easily. This explains why some toddlers cope well in a new and noisy environment, whilst others become irritable and grumpy. By now you will know which stimulus calms your child, and which excites or alerts her. Work within a flexible schedule of awake and sleep times (see age-specific chapters in the second half of the book), so that you will know when to expect your toddler to be tired.

Use calming sensory input to your advantage at sleep time to help calm her down and promote better sleep. Use alerting or stimulatory sensory input when your toddler is in the ***calm-alert state***. This is the best state for learning. Try to help her maintain this state in ***her awake time***. This way, she will interact really well with her world, whilst remaining calm and in control for most of the time.

CALMING VS STIMULATORY OR ALERTING SENSORY INPUT

Certain substances, such as caffeine, are stimulants, and others, such as tranquillisers, calm us down. Our sensory system works much in the same way – some sensory input is calming, such as a deep hug, and other input is stimulatory or alerting, such as being swung around. Some input can even be unpleasant or distressing such as being shaken or swung upside down.

Each of us responds to different types of input in a unique way, and your toddler's responses are dependent on her sensory threshold at the time. Her ability to modulate (balance stimulatory and calming input) depends on her individual neurological threshold and increases with age and as the brain matures. Even though you have an idea by now what calms your toddler down and what hypes her up, here are a few more ideas of how you can use different types of stimulation (either calming or exciting) of the sensory system to your advantage.

Calming stimulation of the sensory system is especially useful if she is over-stimulated. Alerting stimulation of the sensory system can be used to wake her up and/or stimulate her.

Sensory input to either calm or alert your toddler

SENSE	CALMING	HOW?	ALERTING/EXCITING	HOW?
MOVEMENT	Slow, lateral (linear) movements	• Swaying • Rocking in arms or in a rocking chair • Swinging in a hammock or a blanket held by parents • Slow rhythmical swinging on a swing	Jarring, irregular or fast movements such as spinning, rolling and somersaulting	• Fast high swinging or spinning in the air, on slide, merry-go-round or mini-trampoline • Jumping into parent's arms or onto a mattress/cushions • Rolling down a slope • Fast riding on a black bike or tricycle • Hanging upside down over parents legs or a monkey bar
SENSE OF BODY POSITION	Stable positions Resisted movement	• Wrapping tightly in a towel or blanket • Help in the garden, pushing or pulling • Climbing • Wearing a weighted backpack • Pressing down on soap/cream containers to squirt out liquid • Pouring liquids • Using hands: mashing, squeezing a stress ball, playing with Prestik, popping bubblewrap • Eating chewy or crunchy food • Blowing bubbles and whistles	Quick changes in body position, or limbs (some children find this quite painful – this should be looked into – see Appendix A page 129)	• Rough play • Turning upside down • Vibrating toys, cushions or massagers help to alert and balance (The wonderful thing about this type of input, is that it can be used to balance alerting and calming input. So either way, what is listed alongside can be used for either alerting or calming purposes.)

SENSE	CALMING	HOW?	ALERTING/EXCITING	HOW?
TOUCH	Deep pressure touch	• Handle firmly • Deep hugs, especially • Rubbing down with a warm towel after bath • Sleeping under a weighted blanket • Use mattress to make 'people sandwiches'	Unpredictable touch	• Unexpected touch without warning
			Light touch	• Tickling • Blowing onto skin • Differing environment or food textures • Tickly, fluffy toys
	Neutral warmth	• Aid cuddling up in blankets and adapt environment if necessary	Extreme temperatures	• Ice cream with hot chocolate sauce • Play with garden hose or sprinkler • Place ice cubes in a paddling pool of warm water
	Soft and smooth textures	• Soft or silky clothing, bedding and toys • Cuddling up in heavy blankets	Varying textures	• Scratchy clothing (polo necks, collars), bedding or play area • Use textured soap or loofahs in the bath
	Mouthing (touch to mouth)	• Sucking on dummy/ fingers or through straw • Chewing on crunchy food or facecloth or plastic tubing • Licking food off a spoon or ice lollies	Mouthing (touch to mouth)	• Coarse or lumpy food and textures

SENSE	CALMING	HOW?	ALERTING/EXCITING	HOW?
SOUND	Rhythmic sounds	• Classic, nature or baroque music • Humming	Loud noises	• Shouting and screaming • Heavy metal music
	Familiar sounds	• Favourite songs • Ticking of a clock	Unpredictable noise	• Fireworks • Doorbell • Dogs barking
			High pitched noise	• Telephone • Vacuum cleaner
			Fluctuating pitched noise	• Anxious or excited voices • Lawn mower • Musical instrument such as a violin
SMELL	Familiar smells	• Parent's smell • Calming oils such as lavender or vanilla	Pungent, strong smells	• Chemicals • Detergents • Tobacco • Perfume • Paint • Vomit or faeces • Spicy cooking smells • Stimulatory oils such as peppermint
TASTE	Familiar tastes	• Favourite food • Sweet or bland food	Strange or intense tastes	• Sour, salty, spicy or bitter
SIGHT	Natural colours	• Neutral pastel coloured bedroom	Bright, harsh light	• Primary colours • Fluorescent lighting
	Muted light	• Natural or dimmed light	Bright, contrasting light	• Flashing lights • Moving into bright sunlight from indoors

(Table adapted from *Baby sense*)

Keep your face to the sunshine
and you cannot see the shadow

HELEN KELLER

CHAPTER 4

How your toddler signals sensory overload

When Julia is 20 months old, her parents take her to the airport to say goodbye to her grandparents who are returning to their hometown after a visit. Julia helps her granny put her bag in the car, and allows herself to be strapped into her safety seat for the journey. She happily babbles away to her doting grandparents during the drive to the airport, and looks around her with interest. When they arrive she is excited to see the big aeroplanes and sits happily on the luggage trolley, squealing with delight.

Now that you have an understanding of how your child's sensory system works, it is important also to understand that this wonderful and important sensory system can become overloaded very quickly. As your child develops from a chubby one year old to a sturdy pre-schooler, so her sensory system will also develop and mature. If you started your relationship with your child from the word go with an understanding of her signals and her subtle baby talk, you will have been lucky enough to have experienced the rewards of being in tune with her sensory system. However, don't despair, it is never too late to gain insight into how your child's sensory system works, and in particular how she will signal to you when she is in sensory overload.

SENSORY INTEGRATION

The difference between how your one year old and her cousin who is four years old signals sensory load, is quite significant. When your toddler is exposed to sensory input her behaviour will vary depending on how her nervous system interprets the input. All her senses (hearing, sight, touch, smell, taste and the body senses) work together to form a complete picture of what is going on around her.

Sensory integration is the term used to describe the critical function of the brain responsible for producing this complete picture. It is the process whereby sensory input is perceived, processed and a response generated. For most of us, effective sensory integration occurs automatically, unconsciously and effortlessly. Your toddler's nervous system responds to her world either with enjoyment and appropriate interaction to the stimulation, or, when exposed to **excessive** or **distressing sensory stimuli**, by becoming overwhelmed by it, causing her to become irritable and argumentative. Most adults are able to control their environment by removing themselves from the distressing stimulus. To a large degree, your toddler is unable to control her world. She has to communicate her reaction to the stimulus or event to you, so that you, the adult, can help her to feel in control. Your toddler may respond to the stimulus in a number of ways. She may be happy and enjoy the interaction with the stimulus, or she may start to become overwhelmed by it, in which case she will either remove herself from the stimulus (if she is able to), or she may appeal for help. Until she can talk in sentences (generally from the age of two), she may become irritable, aggressive and will eventually begin to cry. She will use her body language to communicate with you.

APPROACH SIGNALS

(Play with me, I am ready for the world)

When Julia arrives at the airport with her family, she has interpreted the stimulation in her world as non-stressful, and responds with many approach signals. These signals show that she is neurologically well-organized, content and is very happy and ready to interact with the world. She is in the calm-alert state.

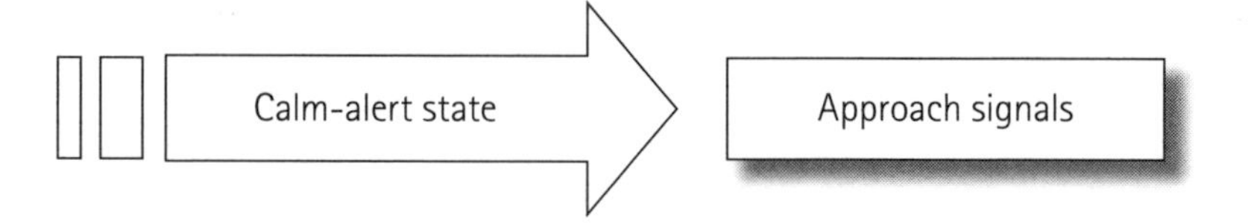

This state is characterised by the following signals:

- She has a relaxed, but alert facial expression, with open eyes. Your toddler will seek eye contact and will stare into your eyes.
- Relaxed body, with smooth body movements (no aimless wandering, flailing arms or running around purposelessly).
- She will turn towards sounds with interest.
- She will turn towards visual stimuli with interest.
- She will ask and respond to questions.
- She smiles and laughs.

This is the state in which your toddler is ready to take in new experiences and learn from her world. Her signals are saying to you, "Interact with me, stimulate me, show me things". This is the best time to talk to, play with and stimulate her, always remembering to have plenty of eye-contact.

WARNING SIGNALS

(Help me, I'm feeling uncomfortable with my world)

After an hour of being exposed to the hustle and bustle of a busy airport, Julia is starting to feel a little overwhelmed and uncomfortable with her environment. She has now moved from the calm-alert state into the active-alert state. She starts to give warning (or self-help) signals to show that she is trying very hard to stop herself from becoming over-stressed by this excessive stimulation in her environment. She has been awake for almost five hours, and is feeling tired. She starts to pick her nose and fidget, and when her mom chastises her, she begins to whine.

Julia is starting to feel a little stressed by all this input, and she will start to behave in a way that will help her dampen the effect of this stress on her nervous system. She acts in a way that is clearly an attempt to stay calm and happy. Now her signals must be interpreted as warning signs that she is approaching overload. She still has some ability to self-regulate (such as picking her nose or fidgeting) and her nervous system is still able to cope at this point but it takes effort.

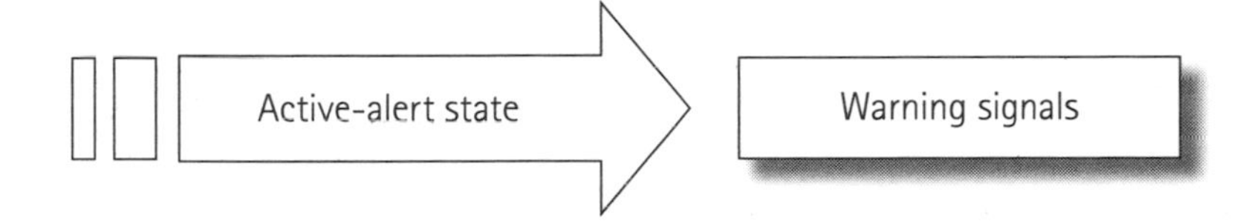

Telling signs are:

- Finger (especially the thumb) or hand sucking
- Decreased eye contact with you
- Excessive mouthing on objects (such as chewing on a straw)
- Nose picking and fidgeting
- Seeking tactile input such as wanting to be picked up
- Whining tone in voice
- Wanting to lie down

Your toddler is giving warning signals, showing you that she is feeling uncomfortable, but is trying very hard to self-calm. If the sensory exposure continues, her nervous system will be pushed into overload, and she will start to whine and become difficult. This is the time to remove her from the stimulating environment, and if necessary allow her to go to sleep.

FUSSING SIGNALS

(Back off – go away – stop all this hustle and bustle)

Julia has tried hard to self-calm, but is no longer able to do so. Her mom is feeling a bit stressed, the plane has been delayed and tempers are short. She has missed Julia's subtle signals to her that she is feeling overwhelmed by the environment, and thinks that Julia's restless behaviour is because she is being naughty. These are clear signs that she needs a sleep or change of environment, and that she is not happy.

If Julia is not able to go to sleep at this point, and made to remain in this stimulating environment, she will become overloaded. She is no longer able to overcome the effect of the sensory input by self-calming. All the sensory input has simply exceeded her ability to cope and her nervous system is now compromised. Julia is not far from bursting into tears and having a tantrum.

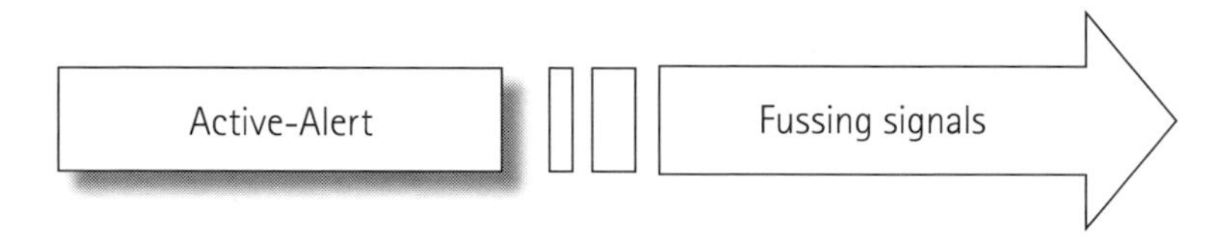

These are the telling signs that she is about to enter the crying state:

- Hand or fingers shielding her eyes
- Loss of eye contact with you, in fact she may stare into space
- Fidgeting
- Frowning
- Yawning or sneezing
- Changes in vital signs such as heart rate and/or respiration, for example, panting with irregular breaths, and you may feel your child's heart beating fast under her shirt
- Moaning or whining
- Demanding a bottle to suck on.

Your toddler is really asking for time out when she shows these signals. It is very important to modify her environment for her, by either removing her from the stimulation, or by removing the stimulation from her.

CRYING AND TANTRUMS

Misinterpreting Julia's signals, her mom tries to cheer her up by putting her on the luggage trolley and whizzing her around. Julia can't understand that her mom doesn't know that this is making her feel worse. When her mom gets cross with her when she protests, it is the final straw. She bursts into tears throws her drink down and stamps her feet angrily, before throwing herself down on the floor. Her parents are confused. Why isn't she appreciating and enjoying this exciting outing? Everyone is staring, and Julia's grandparents look on disapprovingly.

When your toddler is feeling overwhelmed by her environment and is tired, it will not be long before she 'has a tantrum' and cries inconsolably. This is a frustrating and trying time for any parent. If only Julia's parents had read and understood her signals earlier and found a quiet place to sit where Julia could have the time out she needed before the outing ended in tears.

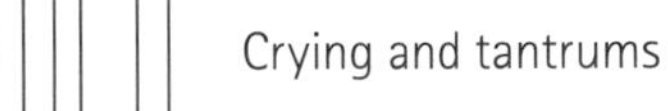

Of course, there are many other reasons for toddlers having tantrums, but overtiredness and sensory overload are two of the main causes of most tantrums. For more about behavioural issues such as tantrums see Chapter 7, page 59.

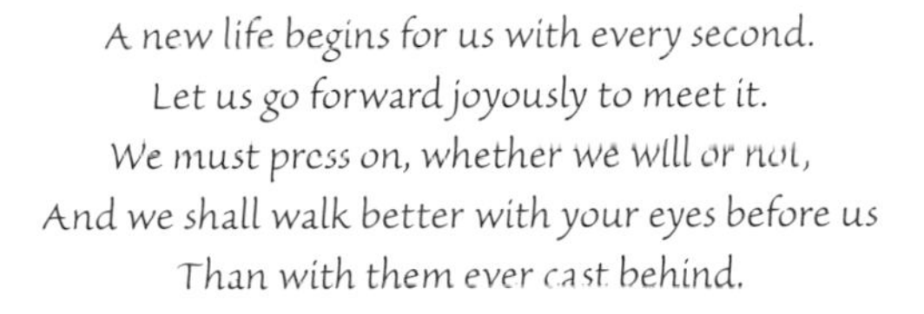

A new life begins for us with every second.
Let us go forward joyously to meet it.
We must press on, whether we will or not,
And we shall walk better with your eyes before us
Than with them ever cast behind.

JEROME K. JEROME

Sleep

CHAPTER 5

After another night interrupted by tears, angry power struggles and frustration, it is hard for Jayne to muster up any feelings of enthusiasm about seeing her son David again in the morning. Jayne feels irritable, frustrated and impatient with David, even though she loves him with all her heart. Now that he is almost 3 years old, she has had enough of these constant night-time battles. She feels exhausted, depressed and burnt out. Her marriage is suffering. When is he going to go to sleep without fighting, and start sleeping the night through?

Establishing healthy sleep habits from the start will ensure that he will fit smoothly into your family's routine. Having enough sleep is as important to your child as following a healthy diet and providing him with adequate stimulation. A well-rested child is less frustrated, more predictable and happier in his world. But your child will not develop healthy sleep habits automatically. He needs a little help from you!

SLEEP CYCLES

It is useful to know a bit about sleep cycles, as this will give you a clearer understanding of your child's behaviour in this context.

There are two different types of sleep – they are divided into light or REM (rapid eye movement) sleep and non-REM or deep sleep. During non-REM sleep we move from drowsiness to light sleep to deep sleep then to very deep sleep quite quickly. Our bodies have very little movement, our heart rate is regular and our breathing slow and even. During REM sleep, we are restless, our eyes move rapidly under closed lids, and our faces may twitch. Our heart rate and breathing may be irregular. Dreaming occurs during this state of sleep, as the mind is very active.

The full sleep cycle, ranging from drowsy through light sleep into deep sleep and then back into light sleep lasts from about 45 to 90 minutes in total. A toddler's cycle lasts approximately 50 to 60 minutes, increasing to about 90 minutes in adulthood. Typically, during a full night's sleep, we pass through sleep cycles many times, drifting back into deep sleep from light sleep, thereby linking sleep cycles resulting in us waking feeling rested and refreshed. The following generally applies with regard to REM sleep:

- Newborns spend about half of their sleeping time in REM sleep.
- Toddlers spend only a third of their sleeping time in REM sleep.
- Adults only spend a quarter of their sleeping time in REM sleep.

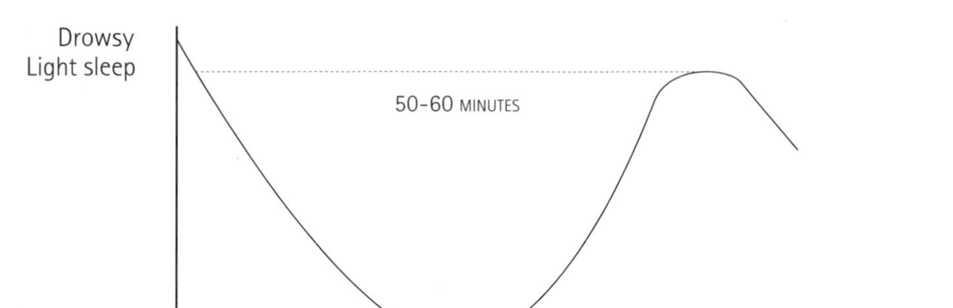

HEALTHY SLEEP PATTERNS

There's no easy answer to the question of how much sleep a toddler needs. However, bear in mind that his ability to be happily awake and happily asleep is determined by his age, his personality, his health, his physical and emotional state but also by appropriate stimulation, coupled with your understanding of his signals to you that he is getting tired. Therefore it is important to be very aware of the duration of his **awake** time.

Even though your toddler has left babyhood behind, he still has limited time periods during which he can be happily awake. As he approaches the end of that time, he should be put to sleep. But if you miss that window of opportunity (where he is tired and ready to fall asleep), he may be able to extend into a 'second wind' where he carries on interacting.

So, when David is still awake at 10 pm at night, seemingly bright eyed and bushy tailed, with high levels of activity, (I call it "Swinging from the chandeliers"), his sensory system is overwhelmed with stimulation, and he is definitely in a state of overtiredness. When he is in this state, adrenalin (a stimulatory chemical in the body) is released – this is to help his body fight the fatigue that he is feeling. Jayne is simply misreading him by thinking that he is not tired, when in fact, sleep is the thing he needs the most. It won't be long before he becomes aggressive, argumentative and weepy, especially about eating and bedtime.

ESSENTIALS FOR EASY SLEEP

There are some requirements to be met with regard to David's emotional state and his sensory system before he is able to fall asleep and stay asleep successfully. He needs to be able to:

- Self-calm after a stimulating day of activities;
- Receive a balanced *sensory diet* of movement stimulation and calming activities;
- Have an ability to screen out noise from the environment;
- Manage fears of dark places and of being alone;
- Be tolerant of limits set by his caregivers around bedtime rituals;

• Be secure enough to separate from his caregiver for sleep.

Studies have shown that poor sleepers do exhibit more daytime behavioural problems and are often seen in conjunction with regulatory disorders such as hyperactivitiy and separation anxiety, which may manifest as defiance, or aggression. However, it is still unclear whether it is the daytime behaviour causing the night-time problems (as is the case with sensory overload), or the night-time battles causing the daytime behaviour (when you have an overtired child who is needy and irritable)! Whichever way, routine, consistency and a structured day go a long way towards solving many behavioural and sleeping problems (more about this later).

Day naps

Don't be fooled into thinking that by keeping your toddler awake all day, an easier night will be had. Depending on the age of your child, a nap during the day is still vital. As your child gets to preschool age (5 years), he will most likely have dropped his regular day nap. However, you will find that he still needs the odd 'power nap' on occasion (usually about once a week) when he has a good sleep to catch up on any sleep debt he may have accumulated. In your younger toddler (1–4 years), watch out for his signals to you in terms of his ***behaviour.*** If you notice that if he wants to skip his day nap but starts to have more and more bad days with plenty of tantrums and fussiness, then he most likely still needs a day nap. If he appears well rested, and is calm and content most of the time, has no problem with bedtime and sleeps well at night, then he is ready to drop his day sleep. (More specific nap times are discussed in the age-specific chapters in the second half of the book.)

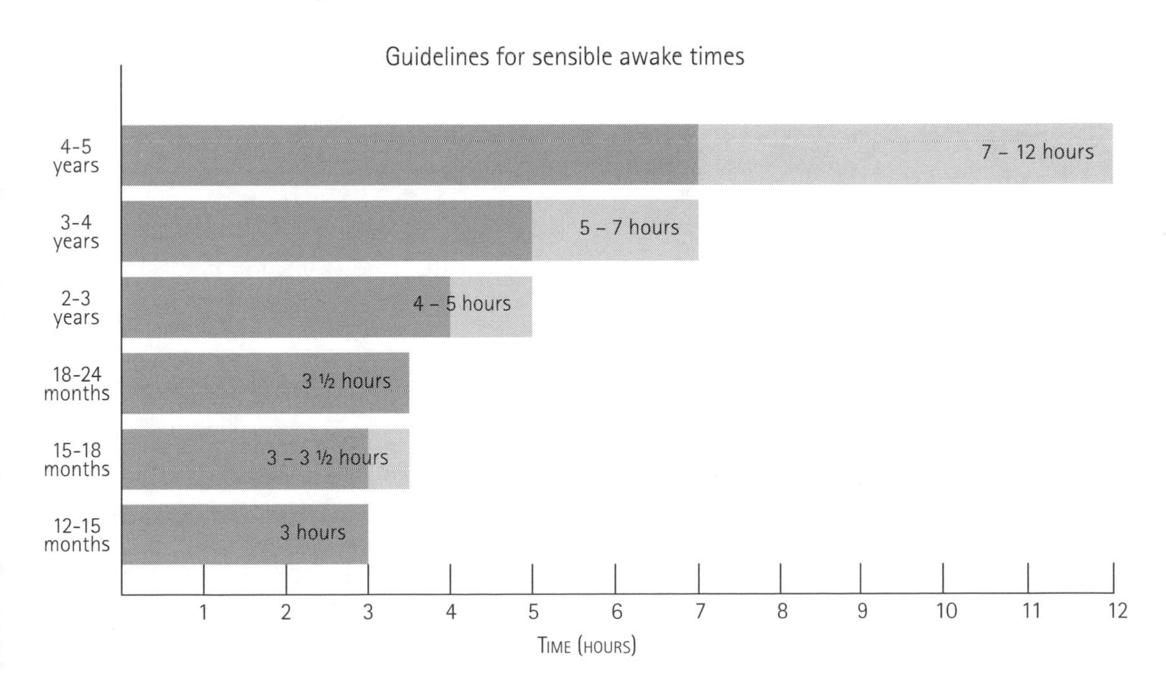

Approximate awake times

If your toddler is having enough sleep, he will wake refreshed and happy, and will have an age-appropriate level of alertness and energy during the day until it is either time for a nap or bedtime.

If he is generally in a calm environment, with the right amount of stimulation (see stimulation ideas in the age-specific chapters), he will be more in tune with his world during the day, and more ready for sleep at night. Over-stimulation during the day, and delayed bedtimes can contribute to sleeping problems and frequent night wakings.

Sleep zone

Whether you have chosen to have your child sleep with you in the family bed, or whether your child sleeps on his own will be determined by your personal beliefs, cultural views and your ability to separate from your child. Either way, choose a sleep zone that suits you.

It is important to regulate your child's environment to ensure that his sleep zone supports sleep. I would recommend that by the time your child is two years old, you try to let him sleep in his own sleep zone. Children need to have their own space, and sleep space is interconnected with physical and emotional boundaries. Encouraging your child to foster some independence from you in the sleep zone paves the way for a sense of security with his own separateness and provides a sound basis for the development of self-esteem and self-reliance. Some ideas for creating a calm and nurturing 'sleep zone' include:

- A darkened room at night (with a dim night light if necessary), and closed curtains for day time naps;
- Special 'sleep friends' such as a stuffed animal or favourite toy;
- A muted colour scheme in his room, avoiding bright or primary colours;
- Avoid menacing posters/wall murals and shelves piled with stuffed animals;
- Don't hang dressing gowns or towels on the back of his door – they can look scary in dim light;
- Avoid glare from a window or a passage or bathroom light;
- If possible, try to keep his play zone in another area of the house, so that he does not associate play with his sleep zone. If it is not possible, pack all toys away before sleep time;
- Keep the cot or bed away from plug points because of electric magnetic radiation.

Bedtime routine

Toddlers thrive on routine, so having the identical bedtime routine every night will soon become a trigger to him to start shutting down to a calmer state. Try to keep this time of the day calm and quiet, so if Dad is home, try to limit the amount of horseplay and excitement that takes place – rather stick to calming, nurturing activities such as watering the garden, doing a puzzle, or playing "I spy".

SLEEP RULES

Dr Mark Weissbluth (MD), founder of the Sleep Disorders Centre at Chicago's Children's Memorial Hospital and a leading researcher suggests these sleep rules:

At bedtime we

- stay in bed;
- close our eyes;
- stay very quiet; and
- go to sleep.

Teach these to your toddler early and repeat them often.

Avoid intensive movement activities and rough house-play at this time, but encourage them earlier in the afternoon. Try to serve supper at roughly the same time each evening, and perform the same activities thereafter until bedtime:

- Tidy up – teach him to put his own dishes in the sink or dishwasher.
- Lay out his pajamas and toiletries on the bed – let him help you – and run his bath. Let him help you, but **never** leave him alone in the bathroom.
- Give him a warm, calming bath, or bath with him – add a drop of lavender or chamomile oil. A few stack toys are ideal for bath time – this is also a nice time for Dad to get involved.
- Wrap him tightly in a warmed towel when you are finished, and dry him with deep, firm strokes. Deep-pressure activities such as this are most useful to help him calm down. Have a favourite song that you always sing at this time (such as "This is the way we dry ourselves ...") or have some calming, lullaby music playing softly in the background.
- A massage (if he will let you) is a wonderful way to end off bath time. Deep pressure touch is, for most of us, one of the most effective ways to calm when we are feeling overloaded. Massage enhances parent-child bonding, helps your child to calm to the quiet alert state, and so promotes deeper sleep. (Contact the International Association of Infant Massage South Africa at tel. (011) 787 0618 for details of an instructor in your area.)
- If there is time before bedtime, keep all stimulation to a minimum. Play quiet games such as puzzles and stacking games, and read stories (no dragon stories!). Try to remain within the sleep zone.
- Offer the last drink of the day, usually a milk drink (if appropriate). Do not offer a drink containing stimulants such as sugar or caffeine (for instance sugary tea or fruit juice).
- Supervise a last trip to the bathroom to brush teeth and wash hands, a nappy change or, if age appropriate, a loo stop!
- Help him to choose a book for his bedtime story (if age appropriate). Then a cuddle and kiss, and into bed – no story unless he gets into bed and under the covers! Read a bedtime story that is age appropriate,

SENSE-ABLE SECRET
It is important to know that it is normal for your child to wake up if he is frightened, ill or when home life is disrupted; these are obviously not sleep problems. At times like this, your child needs comfort, not discipline.

and not too scary – stick to old favourites (toddlers love to hear the same story over and over again). A good tip is to make up an ending that entails the hero/heroine also going to sleep! Try not to get hooked into more than one story.

- Give him a last kiss and cuddle, and a firm and loving "Goodnight!". Leave when your child is still happily awake, not drowsy or asleep. If you don't do this, you'll only create an expectation that you will always stay with him until he is drowsy or asleep, which may become a behavioural issue later.

WHAT HAPPENS WHEN HE DOESN'T SLEEP?

Ask any parents of a toddler who doesn't sleep and they will tell you horror stories about bedtime dramas and nocturnal wakings. Poor quality sleep (for both child and parents) over time results in an accumulation of sleep debt. Sleep debt is simply the amount of sleep that our bodies need over time, but do not get. Lack of sleep or chronic fatigue can lead to poor concentration and memory, decreased creativity, and can make you more prone to accidents. Parents who have not had a good night's sleep in years have been robbed of private time that they need to restore their emotional strength and sanity. Children who are chronically tired may have problems developing self-confidence, feel very anxious and may exhibit behavioural problems such as irritability, aggression, defiance and tantrums. Their sensory system simply cannot cope with this accumulative sleep debt, so any task or activity they undertake is at huge cost to their nervous system.

Signs of chronic sleep debt (deprivation) in a child

- Frequently irritable, argumentative, demanding and clingy.
- Never wakes up happy and rested.
- Rubs his eyes frequently (if you have ruled out allergy).
- May appear to have 'droopy' or puffy eyes.
- May be difficult to wake up in the morning, and will sleep late if given a chance to.
- Age-inappropriate frustration, inattention, impulsivity and hyperactivity.

CAUSES OF SLEEP PROBLEMS

Any stress or change that a toddler experiences may influence his sleep patterns. He may start having difficulty in falling asleep, with many delaying tactics such as asking you to check for monsters or lie with him. He may also start to express a fear of the dark, or things such as dogs or spiders (see Chapter 11: Care and development 2–3 years, page 107). *Sudden* bedwetting, frequent wakings, with or without sleep-walking, nightmares and night terrors and sudden, age-inappropriate dependence on objects such as a dummy or bottle can also be an indication that he may be feeling stressed.

There are many reasons why your toddler may feel stressed, with resulting sleep disturbances.

Changes in his world

Any change in your child's environment may cause a change in his sleep habits. The arrival of a sibling, especially when the new baby is about 3 months old can cause your toddler to become excessively weepy and clingy, especially at bedtime. Try to spend some extra special time alone with him during the day (see page 96, Arrival of a sibling).

Moving into a new home, starting or changing playschool, a change of teacher or caregiver may also cause a problem. Be firm and loving, and know that it will pass.

The death of a parent, grandparent, or loved caregiver, as well as divorce, may also cause sleep disturbances. Acknowledge his loss with him, and allow him time to grieve with lots of extra hugs and kisses – but keep sleep boundaries in place.

If you have returned to work, expect your toddler to be a bit unsettled. Give him time to get used to his new routine.

Holidays, or houseguests can disrupt the routine your child has come to know and expect. Try to keep your routine the same as always, even if you are not at home – toddlers need to know what is coming next, and become very confused when things change.

Separation anxiety

Most toddlers undergo a normal separation anxiety at around the age of 18 months. This may last until they are 2 or 3 years old. Encourage separation games during the day such as peek-a-boo from one room to the other; create a goodbye/sleep book with pictures of yourself kissing him goodnight, then saying hello, and try to stick to the same rituals of saying goodnight. Don't be tempted to slip away without saying goodnight (or goodbye).

Medical and health issues

If you or your child are hospitalised owing to illness or surgery, it will obviously be very traumatic for all concerned – expect your routine to take at least 10 days to settle once you are home.

If your child is ill or teething expect your nights to be a bit wobbly – medicate if necessary.

Certain medication can cause side-effects such as insomnia and hallucinations – so be informed before administering any new medication to your child. Always check ingredients of medicine with your pharmacist.

Worm infestation can also cause restless nights as some worms' eggs are active at night in the anal area, causing irritation and itchiness – consider de-worming your child if he is a very restless sleeper. Remember to de-worm the whole family, including your animals, and check out playschool staff as well.

Speak to your healthcare provider about the correct age-appropriate dosages.
Anaemia can cause behavioural problems and frequent night waking, so speak to your clinic sister or pharmacist about a good iron supplement.
Some children have difficulty regulating their sensory system, which impairs the ability of their nervous system to shut down at sleep time, and to stay in a sleep state for the night (see Appendix A, page 129).

Inappropriate stimulation

Exposure to too much of the wrong sensory stimulation, for example excessive and inappropriate TV watching in the late afternoon and evening, can overstimulate your child's nervous system, impairing his ability to shut down and go to sleep. Rather play some gentle classical music, and keep the TV switched off. Going to bed too late when he is already overtired and in sensory overload can cause bedtime battles and frequent night waking.

Nutrition

Inadequate nutrition, such as malnutrition or excessive intake of sugar, colourants and preservatives, plays an important role too. Make sure that your toddler's diet is varied, with plenty of fresh fruit and vegetables and at least six servings of protein a day (approximately six heaped teaspoons). Limit treats in the afternoon and after dinner!

Difficulty processing stimulation

Poor sleepers typically have difficulty processing stimulation, especially that of touch and movement, and become overloaded very quickly. Occupational therapists often recommend the use of a ***brushing and joint compression technique*** to balance ***alerting and calming*** neuro-chemicals. Brushing your child's body in a certain way with deep and firm strokes using a prescribed brush (which has been well researched) has been shown to promote the maturation of the brain centre that enhances sensory processing and controls the sleep/awake cycle. This technique needs to be carefully monitored and supervised by an occupational therapist qualified in sensory integration, as it can lead to sensory overload, aggression and even further disturbance of sleep if not used judiciously.
So, if you have "tried everything", and your child is still not sleeping, consider having him assessed by an occupational therapist specialised in sensory integration (see Appendix A, page 129) to determine if he has sensory integration problems and needs specialist treatment.

COMMON SLEEP PROBLEMS

Some parents may wonder why their child seems to have such difficulty with sleep issues, when other children seem to sleep like angels. Your toddler may be a bad sleeper if he has chronically poor sleep habits that started in infancy, or his sleep problems may be a new thing for you.

More specific age-related sleep issues are discussed in Chapters 8–12, but let us look at some common ones here.

Drawn out bedtimes or bedtime battles

Your child may draw out bedtime, with numerous delaying tactics and battles which seem to get worse and worse. Common delaying tactics include, "Just one more story?", "Turn the light on, turn the light off!", "No, not this teddy, that one!" and so on. It may last anything from a few minutes to hours! These may be normal developmental delaying tactics, common in toddlers, in which case they will be short lived, or it may be entirely a manipulative behavioural pattern should bedtime boundaries not be clear. Going to bed too late plays havoc with bedtime routines, and is also a major reason for frequent night wakings due to sensory overload.

SOLUTION

Try to aim for a bedtime of between 6 pm and 7 pm. This allows you to be flexible on an 'out of routine day'. So, if you have had a hectic day, resulting in your child missing his nap (depending on his age), rather 'fast forward' your evening routine, and put him to bed at 6 pm. If he has had a good day-time sleep and a quiet afternoon, then 7 pm may be a more appropriate bedtime for that day.

Be very clear about bedtime boundaries (see pages 40–42), and stick to them. So if the rule is, 'Brush teeth before story time, and then it is only one story before lights out', stick to it! Toddlers feel comfortable with boundaries and like to know what to expect. Don't confuse your child with mixed messages every night. Play soft relaxing music or lullabies to help him calm down. See page 72 (age 12–15 months) and page 119 (age 3–4 years) for age-appropriate sleep-training strategies for bedtime battles.

Night wakings

It is important to note that everyone wakes up spontaneously many times during the night. So, even if your toddler is 'sleeping through', the fact is that he is probably waking up at least 4–5 times a night.

Most of the time he will simply stir, turn over or call out, but will be able to go back to sleep. Should he wake fully, he will be able to go back to sleep independently by using comforting and familiar methods that he knows such as finger sucking, holding onto or snuggling down with a security object.

Poor sleepers wake in the same way, but are unable to self-soothe to go back to sleep without some sort of external intervention from a caregiver, such as being stroked or tickled, given a drink or having a parent sleep alongside them. These children have difficulty staying asleep and wake up frequently in the night. Some children simply need reassurance that someone is there, but some may experience nightmares, or even sleep walk (see Special sleep problems, page 44). Many children wake in the night expecting some interaction with a parent, whether it is a drink, a hug, or lying down with them, either in their or their parents' bed. Some children are scared of the dark, whilst others are simply experiencing a normal developmental disequilibrium, such as the excitement of discovering that they can walk.

There are solutions for night wakings.

STOP NIGHT-TIME BREAST FEEDS

As long as weaning is done with a lot of emotional support from all the child's caregivers (parents, nanny and so on), it should not interfere too much with his sleep patterns. However, if he has a sleep association with the breast, he will need plenty of reassurance when he wakes in the night expecting a feed. Stay with him, hold him and rock him until he is asleep (no matter how much he protests). Do this each time he wakes. Offer him sips of water in case he is thirsty. When he is happy to be comforted without a feed, but still needs you to be there, begin sleep training (see page 72 (age 12–15 months) and page 119 (age 3–4 years) for age-appropriate sleep-training strategies). Be firm and loving, and most of all consistent. Remember that unless your toddler is ill, he does not need any nutritional support in the night in the form of breast or any other milk feeds. Also see Appendix C, page 135, on weaning.

GETTING RID OF NIGHT-TIME BOTTLES

Remove the expectation of this middle of the night 'event', and your toddler will no longer wake up for it. Unless they are ill, children from the age of 1 year do not need any nutrition in the night, so there is no nutritional reason for night feeds at this age. If your toddler is used to getting a bottle of milk or juice in the middle of the night, stop offering it, and he will soon stop waking for it. Yes, it is as simple as that! ***It is important to implement sleep training with each waking session no matter how much he protests.***

Have a cup of water on his bedside table and tell him at bedtime that it is there for him if he is thirsty in the night, but that he needn't wake you to tell you he is thirsty! Take him on a special outing to buy his 'special cup' and allow him to fill it himself before going to bed. It is also a good idea to keep a night light on, or fit a dimmer switch so that when he wakes in the night, he will be comforted by his familiar environment, and with a bit of luck, will go back to sleep on his own.

You may have to encourage him to do this himself for the first few nights. If he doesn't settle down, you may have to implement some sleep-training strategies. (See page 72 (age 12–15 months) and page 119 (age 3–4 years) for age-appropriate sleep-training strategies.)

ELIMINATE YOUR CHILD'S DEPENDENCE ON YOU TO GO BACK TO SLEEP

If your toddler is unable to go back to sleep by himself when he wakes in the night, and expects you to interact with him by tickling, stroking or lying with him, the first step is to, once again, ***remove this expectation.*** At bedtime, reinforce the idea of his 'sleep friend' such as a special toy or blanket, and remind him to seek comfort from this object when he wakes in the night. Keep the 'sleep friend' in his sleep zone, and never encourage him to play with this object in his awake time. You could also offer him a security object that smells like you such as a t-shirt or scarf. Keeping a dim night light on his room is useful, as he will be able to recognize his sleep zone and be comforted by it. He will also be able to find his 'sleep friend' and reach out to hug it. At bedtime, always tell him that he is safe and that you love him. When he wakes in the night and simply cries (if he is a young toddler unable to talk and is still in a cot) adopt the sleep strategies as discussed in Chapter 8 (Care and development 12-15 months, page 72). If he is able to talk, and tells you that he needs you to lie with him before he will go back to sleep, adopt the sleep strategies as outlined in Chapter 12 (Care and development 3-4 years, Bedtime battles page 119). *It is important to implement sleep training with each waking session no matter how much he protests.*

SENSE-ABLE SECRET
Let your behaviour do the talking when it comes to sleep – try to avoid the trap of continually negotiating, explaining or threatening.

Obviously if your child is sick, he will need to be comforted throughout the night should he wake. Please do not implement any sleep training or behaviour modification if your child is not well.

SPECIAL SLEEP PROBLEMS

There are special sleep problems that will need a specific approach or special treatment.

Nightmares

Nightmares are part of normal sleep, and are not associated with any specific emotional problems. Nightmares occur when we dream during the REM or light cycle of sleep. If your toddler has a nightmare it is likely that he has been dreaming of normal anxieties and fears, such as falling off a building, or not being able to breathe. In most instances, he may simply call out, but *continue to sleep.* Older toddlers (approximately four years of age) are more prone to nightmares as their imagination can become overwhelming at this stage. If you can hear that he is getting increasingly distressed, then go to him, wake him up and console and calm him.

If your child has many nightmares, keep a dim night light on in his room – he will be comforted by this. Nightmares are usually a passing phase and have no lasting effect on your child.

Night terrors

Night terrors are different to nightmares in that your child *wakes up* (usually screaming). He looks terrified and anxious, his heart is pounding, his chest heaving, and he is utterly inconsolable. Night terrors are not bad dreams, and actually occur when he is sleeping deeply.

There is not much you can do for your child while he is having a night terror other than holding him tightly and reassuring him that you are there. Most night terrors subside after a few minutes. However, research has shown that night terrors are common in children with abnormal sleep schedules. If your child is experiencing night terrors, try to encourage a daytime nap, move his bedtime earlier and avoid excessive stimulation and sensory overload during the day, particularly before bedtime.

Sleepwalking

Sleepwalking is unusual in toddlers, although research has shown that sleepwalking is more common if there is a family history. Some children open and close doors or dress and undress.

There is no treatment, other than ensuring the environment is safe, then gently taking him back to bed, and tucking him in.

Sleeptalking

Some toddlers will mutter and mumble in their sleep – usually simple phrases like "No more!" or "Go away!" as if they were remembering an event that may have occurred during the day. Try to limit over-stimulation, particularly before bedtime. If your child sounds particularly anxious, take note of what is happening in his world during the day, and if necessary, make some changes.

Head banging and body rocking

About 5–10 per cent of children, usually boys, will bang or roll their heads before falling asleep. In most children this is a normal part of development, and should stop by the time they are four years old. This rhythmic behaviour is often due to sensory overload caused by over-stimulation and overtiredness. By moving their bodies rhythmically, the sensory system is calmed, and the children feel calmer and more grounded.

Avoid overtiredness and over-stimulation by encouraging a day nap or some regular quiet time, and move bedtime earlier. Try to encourage your child to participate in more intensive movement and heavy work during the day (pushing a loaded toy/ wheelbarrow and lots of outdoor play). Occupational therapists also recommend placing heavy pressure on your toddler's head and neck towards bedtime. This involves pushing down on the head quite firmly and placing pressure on the neck with a heavy bean-bag on the shoulders. Don't go overboard, though, and preferably use this technique only after a hands-on demonstration by an occupational therapist. Doing it incorrectly could cause more harm than good.

Very rarely, head banging and body rocking are associated with underlying neurological diseases. Your paediatrician will be able to diagnose these uncommon conditions if they are present, so if you are worried, please seek medical help.

Teeth grinding

Teeth grinding during sleep is quite common amongst toddlers, and should improve with age. It has no effect on the quality of sleep, and can occur in any stage of sleep. There is a connection between parastitic infections (worms) and teeth grinding, so if your child grinds his teeth while sleeping, consider de-worming him (see Chapter 11: Care and development 2–3 years, page 111).

Snoring

Research has shown time and time again that children (and indeed adults too) who snore are not getting the best quality sleep. In children this can result in increased incidence of bedwetting, daytime drowsiness, mood changes, hyper-activity, headaches and impaired performance.

A study done at the Children's Memorial Hospital in Chicago suggested that the basis of difficult breathing during sleep (or snoring) was allergies.

If your toddler has two or more of the symptoms below **and** is a difficult sleeper please consult your paediatrician for further advice:

- snoring
- difficult breathing (or stopping breathing) during sleep
- restless sleep
- chronic runny nose
- mouth breathing when awake
- frequent colds or middle ear infections
- sweating when asleep
- poor appetite
- difficulty in swallowing
- excessive day-time sleepiness
- excessive hyperactivity (not age appropriate).

Hyperactivity or sensory overload

Remember those neurotransmitters we talked about in the first chapter? These are the little chemical messengers which are released at each nerve ending as it transmits a message to and from the brain.

The balance of stimulating and calming chemicals enables the sensory system to work efficiently in regulating basic automatic functions of sleeping, feeding, heart rate and breathing. In some children, usually owing to genetic factors, the concentration of the neurotransmitters is faulty, and they give irregular and inconsistent messages to the brain. This can manifest in over-active behaviour. We know too, that disturbed sleep patterns can lead to high levels of these chemicals, which cause the brain (nervous system) to be in a more aroused (alert and wakeful) and irritable state.

This is largely due to stimulatory chemicals being released when the body is fatigued, and, of course, in sensory overload. So, the more tired the child is, the more likely he is to be hyperactive and irritable.

It is easy to see how some toddlers never learn how to fall asleep unassisted – because their parents are not in tune with their toddler's sensory system. These toddlers accumulate a chronic sleep loss over time. And we now know that this long-lasting fatigue in fact, 'turns them on/hypes them up', making them more active by day and by night, which in turn pushes them into a more aroused, alert, irritable and wakeful child. These heightened arousal (or alertness) levels cause even more disturbed sleep, and so the cycle continues. It is very easy for tired and anxious parents to perpetuate this cycle unknowingly.

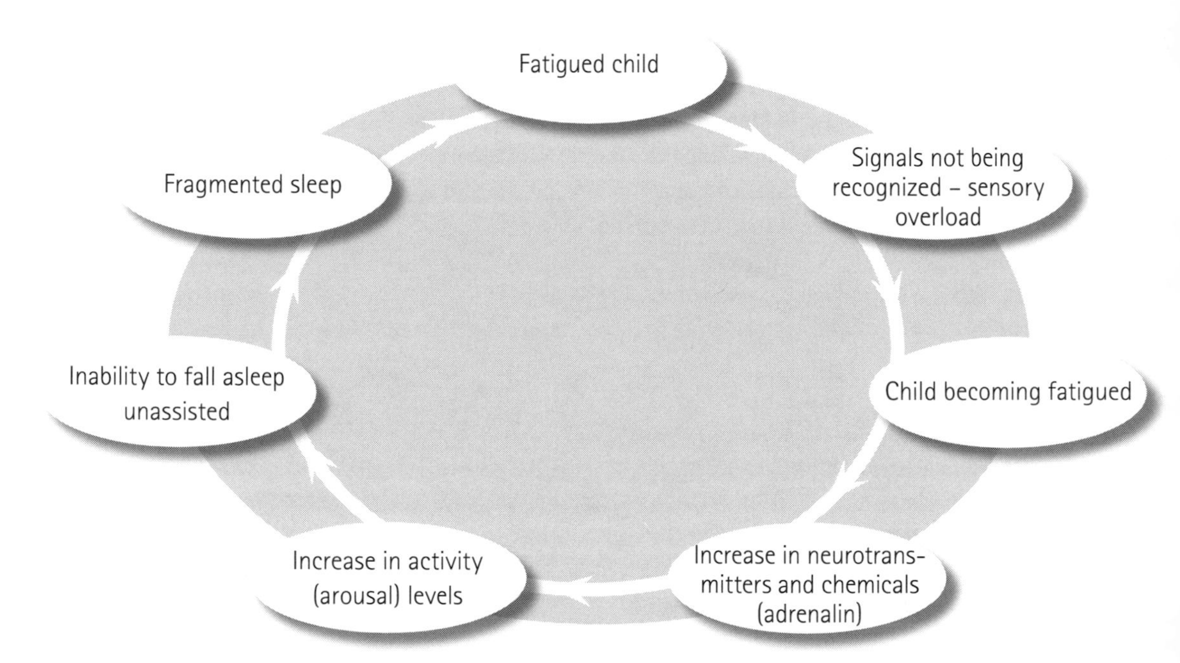

THE SOLUTION

Being in tune with your toddler's sensory system and watching and understanding his signals to you is the first step towards better sleep. Structure and routine, early to bed and teaching him healthy sleep habits will really help calm down a busy or 'hyperactive' child.

You can't break a bad habit by throwing it out the window.
You've got to walk it slowly down the stairs.

MARK TWAIN

Toilet or potty training

CHAPTER 6

Leanne's mom Sue is worried. She has just returned from Leanne's toddler group where the morning's conversation revolved around potty training. Sue is sure that Leanne isn't ready to begin toilet training as she is only 21 months old. However, some of the other moms in the group are quite adamant that 18 months is the correct age, and have already begun to train their toddlers. Leanne is showing no signs of being ready, and has little awareness of what is happening down below in her nappy until it is all over. She plays with her potty and loves walking around with it upside down on top of her head. Sue is worried that she will be hampering Leanne's development if she doesn't start to push her now.

Bladder and bowel control can only occur once the nerves and muscles involved are fully developed. This occurs at approximately 24 months of age. Your toddler will begin to make the connection between her inner sensations (via her sensory system, through interoception, see page 17) and the physical reality of passing a stool or urine. The nerves to the bowel and bladder need to get messages from the brain (via the sensory system) to the muscles of the bladder and bowel so that effective emptying can take place. The muscles of the bowel and bladder also need to be strong enough to hold onto their contents until they can be emptied. Some children do have motor control problems, so may take longer to develop control of the sphincter (the valve at the opening of the bladder). Some children are under-reactive to sensations, so may not even notice that they are urinating till much later. On the other hand, if your toddler is over-reactive to sensation, the feeling of something leaving her body may be intense and frightening. Your toddler may simply not enjoy the feeling of sitting on the potty or toilet, after having become accustomed to having the closeness and warmth of the nappy to push against.

DEVELOPMENTAL REQUIREMENTS

For optimal control, it is obvious that your toddler needs to be able to sit, stand and walk in order for this function to take place. She also needs to be able to follow simple instructions, so obviously you will need the full co-operation of your child in order to succeed. You should therefore not feel pressurised to rush into toilet training from an early age (definitely not under 18 months of age), otherwise it is doomed to fail. Two years of age is a good time to begin to prepare your toddler for this big milestone in her life. Most children are indifferent to their bodily functions, so it is a good idea to accept this and follow their cues. What is amusing to note is that around this age (24 months), when most children are developed enough to ***begin*** to gain control of their bowel and bladder function, a strange paradox occurs. Their 'lower end' becomes ready, but at around the same time, the 'upper end' becomes unwilling, as this is the typical age of wilfulness and stubbornness, so your toddler will often resist your sudden interest in her bodily functions! Keep a level head and a sense of humour and all will be well.

THE SENSORY SYSTEM INDICATES READINESS

Sue decided to trust her instinct and hasn't begun toilet training. She is secretly relieved to discover at the following month's toddler group that none of the other toddlers have been successfully toilet trained yet. In fact, one of Leanne's little friends has started to wake up in the night, moaning and shouting, "No potty, no potty!".

Because it is easier to 'hold onto' stools than it is to a full bladder, your toddler will most likely achieve bowel control first. However, it doesn't mean that anything is wrong if bladder control is achieved first.

The first sign that your toddler is ready to become toilet trained, is when she begins to show awareness of what is happening either before or after a bowel movement. She may understand and say words such as 'pooh', 'wee' or 'toilet', squirm and touch her bottom, or may stop what she is doing. If she takes her nappy off continuously, and can pull her pants down, it may be a sign that she is getting ready for this big milestone in her life. The connection is finally there! Her sensory system is giving her the message that something is happening. It is also prudent to take note of the climate at the time that your child may be ready for toilet training. It is far easier to let your toddler potter around the garden completely naked in hot summer months, than in the middle of winter! Having to change countless pairs of corduroys and change socks and shoes each time she has an accident is frustrating and tiresome. If your toddler is younger than 26–28 months in winter, delay toilet training until the weather improves, if possible. Don't leave it too late however, as delaying training for too long can make it worse.

PRACTICAL AND HEALTHY GUIDELINES

Toilet or potty training can be as easy and relaxed as you make it. Not putting any pressure on your little one to perform at any stage improves your chances of success dramatically. Follow these practical suggestions:

- It is a good idea to get a potty well before you think you may need it. Place it in the bathroom near the toilet, and explain what it is even if your toddler is not yet ready.
- Let her accompany you to the toilet from an early age, so that she can get used to the idea, and learn from watching you – this will take the mystery and fear out of this new idea. Always tell her, "Mommy is having a wee". Invite her

to tear off the toilet paper for you, and help you flush.

- If you have a son, ask your husband to invite him to accompany him to the toilet. This way, he will learn that boys do it differently to girls. Place a piece of toilet paper in the bowl and show him how to aim at the paper. If he prefers to sit down to pass urine, reassure him that it is fine and try to avoid putting pressure on him to do it 'the right way'.
- Some children prefer to sit on the 'big' toilet as they find sitting on a potty uncomfortable. Either way, it does not matter whether you start your child off on a potty or on a toilet. If your child prefers to sit on the toilet, invest in a special toddler inner toilet seat (available at most baby shops and supermarkets) for a more comfortable and stable sit.
- If your toddler is frightened by the noise of the toilet flushing, wait until she has left the room before flushing. Always encourage her to help you flush, but if she doesn't want to, don't force her.
- If your child gets 'stage fright', try turning on the taps – the sound of running water may help her relax.
- Teach your daughter how to wipe from front to back, and your son to wait till the drips stop.
- Make it a rule that the toilet seat always goes down after finishing on the toilet.
- Teach your children by example that their hands must be washed and dried after a potty or toilet session, regardless of success or not!
- Consider singing a special song such as, "This is the way we go to the loo, go to the loo, go to the loo..." to encourage reluctant toddlers to co-operate. Story books explaining what is happening are also most useful.
- Expect some regression if she is stressed in any way such as starting a new school, the arrival of a sibling or illness. Let her go back into nappies, and with loads of love and encouragement, try again after a short while.

SENSE-ABLE SECRET

Invest in a toilet seat with an inner and a built-in step and hand rail. This way, your toddler will be able to sit comfortably on the toilet and will always have her feet on a firm surface as well as have something to hold on to.

GAINING BOWEL CONTROL

If your toddler is able to indicate to you that she is *about* to have a bowel motion, then you can suggest a visit to the bathroom where she can sit on the toilet or a potty. Adopt a matter of fact and casual approach, and if she refuses, don't push the issue. Try again in a few days. If she succeeds, praise her without going overboard – she needs to know that this is a normal, routine function and is nothing special or out of the ordinary. If she fails, make no mention of it, and replace her nappy in the usual way.

If she indicates to you that she has ***already had*** a bowel motion, then change her nappy in the usual way, whilst reinforcing the words she may have uttered at the time ('pooh', 'stinky' and so on). This will help her to connect the sensation with a word. Encourage her to tell you these words when she feels the sensation. With a bit of luck, she will start telling you earlier and earlier each time. Never scold or admonish her if she doesn't tell you in time.

Encouraging the use of the toilet or potty to gain bowel control first is a sensible way to begin toilet training as most children are fairly predictable in their bowel movement (usually after a meal, or bath-time), so you can be more prepared.

GAINING BLADDER CONTROL

This is a much more gradual process, as her bladder will have to become more and more capable over time of holding larger quantities of urine. This too, generally occurs closer to the age of 24 months (or later), when the muscles of the bladder are stronger. She may indicate to you in much the same way as she does when she has already urinated. She may say 'wee wee', squirm or tug at her nappy. Change her nappy as usual, and re-enforce the words she uses whilst doing so. When you notice that her nappies are remaining drier and drier over time (for example when she has a daytime nap), or when she is in the region of 24 months old, you can begin leaving the nappy off during the day for periods of time. Take her shopping for new underwear, and allow her to choose them herself. 'Pull up' nappies with elastic are also very useful. Use your common sense when allowing her to go without a nappy. So, when you are home with her leave the nappy off but outings or sleeps will still be nappy time. When she is only wearing underwear (without a nappy), ask her frequently (about every 40 minutes) if she would like to wee. Invite her to come with you to the bathroom, and let her copy your actions. Praise her if she manages to pass urine, but don't make a huge fuss – she needs to learn that this is a normal part of life. If nothing happens, ignore the event. If she has an 'accident' on the lounge carpet 2 minutes after this ritual, don't make a fuss. Say something in a very matter of fact tone such as, "Oh dear, you had a spill. Don't worry, let's mop it up together". Never shout at her or scold her; it is not her fault. Her sensory system may still need a bit more time to mature to get the right messages through, or her bladder muscles may need some more time to strengthen. Keep going with the training, and you will see that with time and perseverance, the connection will finally happen when her bladder will send the correct message to her brain in time, and she will be able to wait comfortably until she gets to the bathroom.

IT'S AN ACCIDENT!

Tell your toddler in a firm, loving and sympathetic way that accidents do not matter, that they are forgotten about and forgiven instantly and that she is not to worry about them.

ACHIEVING DRY NIGHTS

By the age of four years most children are dry at night. The first sign that your night nappies may soon be a thing of the past, is when your toddler is able to control her bladder for a few hours during the day.

When she has at least seven dry nappies in a row overnight, you can remove her night nappy. This may take anything from a few days to a few months to achieve, so don't rush things. Expect the odd accident, especially if she is under emotional stress for any reason. Keep a waterproof sheet on the bed for at least another year just in case.

LATE DEVELOPERS

All children develop at their own pace. The same can be said for toilet or potty training. Some gain control of their bladder and bowel sooner or later than others. This doesn't mean that anything is wrong. Research has shown that boys are generally slower than girls to attain bladder and bowel function control, and that there is often a family history. Most children have mastered potty or toilet training during the day by the time they are three years old.

If you are struggling to toilet train your toddler and she has any of these symptoms, please consult your doctor or healthcare professional for further follow up:

- Blood stained urine or faeces;
- Pungent or strong smelling urine that may look cloudy;
- Persistent redness, itchiness or swelling around the genital and rectal area;
- Chronic diarrhoea or constipation.

BED WETTING

Bed wetting is more common in boys, especially after the age of four years. However, many children, whilst remaining dry during the day, wet their bed every night. Try limiting the amount of fluid your toddler drinks for 1–2 hours before bedtime, and encourage a trip to the toilet as the last thing before lights out. 'Lift' your toddler later on in the evening when you go to bed. This entails placing her on the toilet half asleep and encouraging her to wee. Most children comply and go back to sleep quickly, and remain dry till morning. I would not recommend this if you have a poor sleeper. If necessary, keep night time nappies for as long as it takes until they are dry at night. Surprisingly enough, most children are unfazed about having a night nappy and just accept it as part of their normal routine. Remember to always keep a waterproof sheet on the bed.

When bedwetting is a new behaviour (when your toddler has been dry at night for a period of time already), it is most likely due to some sort of emotional upset such as starting a new school, the arrival of a new sibling, or illness. Don't make a fuss and offer her loads of reassurance that it's not her fault, and that it will improve with time.

It is always a good idea for your toddler to have a full medical check up if she is still wetting her bed at night and is older than five years, to rule out any underlying problems such as infection. If the muscles of the bladder are affected, medication is prescribed in some cases to aid muscle control. Some children have a deficiency of antidiuretic hormone (ADH). This hormone concentrates the urine thereby reducing the amount of urine in the bladder so that it does not overfill whilst asleep. Some children respond well to a special alarm that goes off when the first drop of urine is detected in the bed. This wakes the child up so that she can go to the toilet. This method helps train the muscles of the bladder to strengthen.

REFUSING TO HAVE A BOWEL MOVEMENT IN THE TOILET

It is fairly common for some toddlers to refuse to have a bowel movement on the potty or in the toilet. She will demand a nappy to be put on, and will invariably go to a private spot (usually behind the couch or wrapped up in the curtains) and do it there! Some toddlers refuse to 'go' on a strange toilet, or if there are visitors in the house. The best way to handle this is to comply with her request, and treat it as completely normal. With lots of patience and encouragement it should settle on its own within a few months. But if it starts to become a problem and encroaches on her enjoyment of activities, it may be time to do something about it.

Wait until she is calm, content and happy and when you have lots of time to be with her. If she likes to hide away while she has a bowel movement, encourage her to go and hide in the bathroom and to help you dispose of it once she is finished. If she goes at a certain time of the day, take her to the bathroom and encourage her to pooh in her nappy there. If she gets this right, you are making good progress. Once she is able to have a bowel movement on schedule in the bathroom (but still in the nappy), move to the next step. Bear in mind that this may take some time. Be patient.

When she says she wants to pooh, allow her to keep her nappy on, but encourage her to sit on the toilet. The next day, loosen the nappy a bit until it is just under her, but not on her. If she gets this right (even if the nappy is still on) you are making good progress. Move onto the next step.

Hide away all her nappies, so she cannot see them. When she asks for a nappy, tell her that the nappies are finished. Gently guide her towards the toilet or potty, making sure that her feet are supported to make her feel more stable and to help her regulate her body. Offer to sit right beside her or just outside the door for as long as it takes. Be very careful not to pressurise her as this can make it worse. Have your book handy and offer her one too. She may like to hold a favourite toy. It sometimes helps to encourage her to play out the process, so let her place her doll over a toy potty. Be sure to acknowledge and empathise with both her and her doll's feelings at the time. ("I know that you and your dolly don't want to sit on the toilet, and I know that it is difficult for you, but it is OK to feel a bit scared.")

Let her know that she is under no pressure and that you are calm and non-plussed by the event. Play some calming music and let the taps run slowly.

Bear in mind that she shares your desire to master this 'grown up' behaviour, but she may have fears of disappointing herself. Give her the space to express these feelings when you have your special floor-time with her during the day (see Chapter 8: Care and development 12–15 months, page 74).

Constipation

Another problem that stems from 'holding it in', is that your toddler may become constipated. The harder the stool (from holding it in), the more painful it is to pass, and the more reluctant your toddler will be to go to the toilet. If this is the case, make sure that she drinks plenty of water and eats enough fruit and vegetables. If her stools remain hard and difficult to pass, speak to your pharmacist or doctor about a gentle laxative to help soften the stool. Do not use laxatives for longer than prescribed.

WHEN TO SEEK HELP

If your doctor has ruled out any cause of delayed toilet training or persistent bed wetting, and your child is older than four years of age, consider consulting a paediatric occupational therapist trained in sensory integration therapy (see Appendix A, page 129).

From success you get lots of things,
but not that great inside thing
that love brings you.

SAM GOLDWYN

Behaviour and discipline

CHAPTER 7

Kieran (3 years) appeared to be having a wonderful time. It was his cousin's fifth birthday, and the family had gathered at their local 'kiddy friendly' restaurant for a celebratory lunch. As it was a safe zone for him to play in, his parents largely ignored him as he happily ran around chasing his cousins, jumped on the mats and shrieked with glee. When he threw himself on the floor and screamed loudly when refused an ice-cream, his mother Meghan, was mystified as to how quickly he had changed from a happy, toddler to this inconsolable, difficult child. When Kieran kicked his granny in the stomach and lashed out across the table sending two glasses flying, his mom realized it was time to go home. Kieran refused to say goodbye to anyone, and put up a fight when he had to be strapped into his car seat. The family outing was ruined, Kieran's parents could sense the rest of the family's disproval, and the drive home was fraught with tension. Kieran was argumentative and clingy when they got home and it took a long time for him to eventually settle down and have a nap.

Everybody loves a happy, smiling and friendly child. These 'fun' emotions are easy for everyone to handle. However, when the dark side of your toddler emerges, it becomes more difficult to manage.

No one knows better than you that your toddler is able to do a lot more now than he could when he was a baby. He wants to learn and discover more about this new and exciting life of his, but explodes with rage when he realizes that he still needs help in this new-found quest for independence! A child, just like an adult, will experience a range of different emotions in the course of each day. By not having the right words to express his anger, confusion, fear or insecurity, your toddler may signal his distress in non-verbal ways such as tears, wailing and flailing arms and legs. In some instances he will be so frustrated that he may push or bite another child. With sensitivity and consistency, you will be able to teach your child that all *feelings* are okay, but not all *behaviours* are.

TEMPER TANTRUMS

Seemingly bad behaviour and temper tantrums seem to go together. Your delightful child suddenly stamps his feet defiantly if he can't get his own way, or flies into a rage for no apparent reason. Temper tantrums are a necessary and healthy (but difficult) part of growing up.

Toddlers have a low level of frustration – temper is easily triggered when things don't go according to plan. In younger toddlers (under the age of 3), most tantrums are caused when they become frustrated with their inability to perform certain tasks, such as putting on their own shoes. This is when a helping hand, not punishment, is all that is needed, and the tantrum soon abates.

If your four-year-old uses a tantrum to deliberately defy your authority, then something must be done about this (see page 61).

Sensory overload

It is important to remember that overtiredness and over-stimulation leading to sensory overload, also contribute towards temper tantrums and bad behaviour. It is especially worse in public situations, where unfamiliar people, loud noise, bright lights and different smells are too much for your toddler to handle. He will also know that he does not have your full attention in a public setting, so will play up in order to get it!

If only Kieran's mom had realized that it was getting close to Kieran's nap time, the day might have ended on a happier note. Kieran would most probably have accepted the fact that he couldn't have an ice cream had he not been overtired and fractious by then. Kieran hadn't eaten his lunch as he was too busy playing, so he was most likely feeling hungry as well. Meghan assumed that Kieran was missing her when he insisted on cuddling on her lap even though the other children were still playing, and hadn't noticed Kieran pushing over his younger cousin. Kieran had simply become totally overwhelmed by his environment, and from having started out in the calm-alert state when they arrived, had moved quickly into the active-alert state once he became stimulated by his surroundings. As his environment was not controlled in any way, he soon became over-stimulated. This over-stimulation, coupled with the fact that he was hungry and tired, soon led to tears.

Be one step ahead

If you know what signals to look for and ensure that you are in tune with your toddler's sensory signals, you can remain one step ahead and avoid temper tantrums.

- Modulate the stimulatory environment or remove your child from it if you see any signs of overload (see pages 31-34).
- Watch awake times – try to plan outings and activities during your child's awake times to avoid tantrums and tears (see page 75).
- Be consistent. Try to stick to a routine. Routine is important to toddlers – it gives them boundaries and predictability in their world, which helps them feel secure. For more information about boundaries, keep reading!
- Avoid hunger. Your toddler needs to eat frequently, so don't let him get too hungry – he will become very grumpy.

- Prevent a situation from arising: If you see that your two-year-old is struggling to put on his shoes and is getting frustrated, step in and offer to help him before he loses his temper.
- Offer him choices whenever possible. Instead of saying, "Eat your beans", rather say, "Would you like beans or squash?"
- Try to choose your battles – is it really the end of the world if your toddler goes out with two different shoes on?

Tackling temper tantrums

As a parent, it is always important to help your child make sense of what is happening and how he is feeling. This way, your toddler will learn to trust his feelings and solve many of his own problems.

ACKNOWLEDGE HIS FEELINGS

Try to get into the habit of always acknowledging how your child is feeling by giving his feeling a name, then mirror the feeling, then offer some sort of distraction. For example, when Kieran started to perform when refused his ice cream, his mom might have tried handling it in a different way. She could have said, "Oh dear, are you cross that you can't have an ice cream? I would be too if I were you because you are so tired, but I tell you what, let's go and have a look at the balloons and see if they have a blue one – that's your favourite colour, and then we'll go home for a sleep." This way, your child will get the message from you that whatever he is experiencing is not dangerous, not out of control and can be managed.

STAY CALM

Stay calm in the storm of the tantrum! Your role is to contain his distress, so don't stomp out of the room, try not to shout if he shouts, or be angry if he is angry (this will only lead to two toddlers in the room!) If your toddler will allow you, help him to sort out what it is that is causing his frustration (such as not finding the right hole for the shape he is playing with). If it is too late for that, give him a big, firm and deep hug, and try to keep him close to you in this way until his anger subsides. Try to stay with him even if he won't let you touch him, and offer that cuddle later when he is calm. The storm of emotion he is going through can be frightening for him, so he needs to know that you are there for him.

> SENSE-ABLE SECRET
> *Temper tantrums are common and easy to handle – just keep calm and wait it out.*

STAND YOUR GROUND

Don't give in to the tantrum – if you do this you will only be reinforcing the negative or bad behaviour. By conceding, you will only be teaching your child that all he needs to do is have a 'frothy' in order to get what he wants. It is best to ignore the behaviour, and rather focus on the ***reason*** for the tantrum in the first place. By ignoring the tantrum (this may be difficult to do sometimes, particularly if you are in a public place), you are giving him the message that this behaviour does not move you, and he will most likely stop. In the throes of a tantrum, never plead, beg or negotiate – it will give your child the message that you are anxious and not in control.

CREATE DISTANCE

Walk away if you feel that you are losing control – take some deep breaths and count to ten, then return.

Use 'time out' (if the tantrum warrants it) from the age of two years. This is discussed in detail on page 64.

GIVE PRAISE WHERE DUE

Always remember to praise and acknowledge your child when he has handled a difficult situation well, or if he has done as you have asked. This way, you only reward positive behaviour, and largely ignore the negative behaviour. For example, if you see that your child is heading towards a tantrum, use some of the above strategies, and if the tantrum is diffused, you could say to him, " I could see that you were getting frustrated with those shoelaces, but you managed not to lose your temper. Well done, come here for an extra special hug, I'm proud of you!"

IT GETS EASIER

By the age of four years, most toddlers have learnt that there are other, easier ways of getting what they want, so you will notice that temper tantrums will become less frequent.

DISCIPLINE

Testing limits and watching how you react is your toddler's way of establishing a secure understanding of his world. Discipline is an inevitable part of parenting, and is not something that your child is born with. It goes without saying that babies do not need to be disciplined (perhaps it is the parents who do!) However, as your child begins to explore his world more as he becomes mobile, it is important to start setting some boundaries for behaviour – for your sanity, and for his safety. Discipline is not about instilling in children fear of their parents or of home, or about controlling your child's behaviour. It is rather about teaching him the necessary skills needed for self-control, and to help him take responsibility for his own behaviour. Discipline is also about establishing and applying certain age-appropriate rules. However, there are also some rules that *you*, as the parent or caregiver, should try to adhere to. These simple rules will help you to discipline effectively and appropriately.

Boundaries

Setting age-appropriate limits is the cornerstone of discipline. Your child is still small, so keep the rules clear, simple to understand and don't have too many of them – he will never remember them all. Bear in mind that boundaries will move depending on the age of your child. For example, your 15-month-old toddler does not understand that cupboards are not for playing in, but a four-year-old can understand that certain cupboards are out of bounds.

Repetition

It is tough for a toddler to grasp the concepts of taking turns, following instructions and delaying gratification. These are concepts only learned through constant repetition on your side, and practice on his side. Your toddler may literally need to hear something two hundred times, for example, "Do not climb on the burglar bars!" in order for him to finally learn not to do it anymore. This is how toddlers learn how to modify their behaviour. By constantly repeating the rules to him he will, with practice, learn them.

Distraction

Repeatedly denying your toddler 'his way' can convey to him that his individuality is not recognized or acceptable. You will sometimes feel that all you seem to say is, "No!" or "Don't!", but be patient and persevere; it will pay off in the long run. It often helps to offer positive alternatives. For every "no", try to offer a "yes". If he wants to climb on the burglar bars, say, "No, you cannot climb on the burglar bars because your foot can get stuck. Let's go outside and you can climb on the jungle gym." And for every "don't", offer a "do". If he is scribbling on the wall, offer him big sheets of paper for his artwork instead.

When he wants to do something that is a 'no-no' in your family, such as jumping on the bed, it may be better to redirect his attention to rather jump on the trampoline. Using distraction to offer alternatives and letting him learn to find his own alternatives to certain behaviours that you don't allow, will nurture a good sense of independence and self worth.

Tuning in to sensory signals

Being in tune with your toddler's sensory signals (see pages 31–34) will help you to be alert to his moods which in turn will help you to avoid difficult situations. Toddler-proof his environment as best you can, so that most temptations are out of sight. This will help you to avoid getting caught in the endless "No!", "Don't!" cycle.

Be positive

The most effective way to encourage good behaviour is to praise, truthfully, your child for any good behaviour, for example, "Thank you for sharing with Tammy, I liked that". Any acknowledgement, even if it is just a hug, will make him feel good about himself, and will encourage him to repeat the behaviour next time. Negative attention, instead of punishing bad behaviour, actually increases the prevalence of the bad behaviour as your child sees your response as a reward (even if it is a negative response). For example, when you are on the phone and your child is behaving and playing quietly, you ignore him. The minute he starts to perform and misbehave, you shout at him to be quiet. What are you doing? You are telling him that when he is good you will ignore him, but when he misbehaves, he will get your attention. Remember that for some children, any attention is better than none.

Try to distract your child with something interesting if he starts to play up whilst you are on the telephone. Better still, save your calls for when he is asleep, or cut short your call if possible.

Walk your talk

Mean what you say, and say what you mean. If your rule is no chocolate before supper, then stick to it, no matter how fierce the battle! If you relent for the sake of peace and quiet, your toddler will learn that all he needs to do is have a tantrum, and he will get his own way.

Have routines

Toddlers love to know what is happening next, and feel comforted by daily rituals. If your child is used to brushing his teeth every night before bed, then the chance of a battle of wills taking place at bedtime will be greatly reduced.

Pick your fights

Be absolutely sure why you are saying no (again!). Try to turn a blind eye to minor irritations and age-appropriate naughtiness. So if your toddler refuses to take off his slippers at bedtime and wants to wear them to bed, is it really the end of the world? When it comes to matters of health and safety (such as being strapped in a car seat), then the rules are non-negotiable.

Use time out appropriately

Time out is a useful tool to use for a slightly older toddler (from 2 years onwards) who uses a tantrum to openly defy your authority, or displays a behaviour that he knows is not acceptable (such as kicking the dog). Wait until he can understand that rules need to be followed, so that he will understand why time out is necessary.

Time out must not be seen as punishment. It should rather be seen as an opportunity to teach your toddler how to cope with his feelings of frustration and anger. Once he has learnt how to cope with these feelings, he will be able to start to modify his behaviour.

COOLING OFF

If your toddler is still young (1–2 years), start by taking time outs together. So when he starts to push beyond his borders and is getting hyped up, say, "Let's stop for a while, take a deep breath and have some quiet time together". This is a good way to get him used to a 'cooling off' period.

TIME-OUT ZONE

Once your toddler is two years old, he will start to understand a bit more of action and consequence, as well as be able to follow instructions. This is the ideal time to start using more formal time out, if necessary. A good idea is to use his bedroom as the time-out zone.

Remember that if he needs some time out in the first place, his sensory system is most likely overloaded, making him feel out of sorts and disorganised. His bedroom is a safe and secure zone that he is comfortable with, so it will comfort and calm him. Avoid using bathrooms or naughty corners. These areas may make him feel embarrassed, uncomfortable and insecure.

BE CALM, BUT FIRM

When he needs some time out, tell him very firmly that you do not like what he is doing, and that he needs to go to his room. Try not to shout – all that does is reinforce a spiral of negative behaviour. Use your body language to reinforce how serious you are.

Point towards the bedroom, and coax him along. Don't be tempted to smack. If he digs his heels in, pick him up firmly (even if he is kicking and screaming), and take him to his bedroom. Once you are there, say to him, "It's not nice to pinch your sister. Stay here until you feel better". Walk out and close the door. Because he is a toddler, he will weep and wail and may even bash on the door with frustration.

GO BACK TO HIM

Wait for about a minute before you go back. Don't leave him for too long, but don't rush back in immediately – allow him some time to calm himself down. When you re-enter his room, take no notice of the mess that he may have caused; rather keep your voice calm and controlled.

Suggest a cuddle on your lap. If he resists, say calmly, "OK, I will come back in a little while when you are feeling better". Leave the room for another minute. Go back in and repeat your offer. Continue in this way until he is ready for a hug and a cuddle. Sit on the floor, or his bed or a chair in his room, and hold him firmly with a deep hug. Singing a favourite song is also most useful. Wait until he is calm.

NAME HIS FEELING

Briefly discuss the event that caused the time out in the first place. Remember to always *acknowledge and name* how he is feeling by saying, "I know that you are feeling angry because I sent you to your room", then *mirror* the feeling by saying, "I would also feel angry if I were you", then ***explain why he was sent to his room*** by saying, "It wasn't very nice to pinch your sister. So remember that next time when you are feeling frustrated with her, pinching is not the way to deal with it".

Suggest that he puts the 'bad thought' into a little box or an imaginary bubble, then go with him to the bedroom window and empty the box, or blow the bubble away. Offer to help him tidy up his room (if he has trashed it in his rage), then continue with your activities. Reassure him that time out doesn't mean that you don't love him, and that you will always love him no matter what. Don't refer to the episode again – not even when dad comes home from work – it is over. This method can be used up to school-going age.

Discipline in public places

Obviously time out will work if you are at home. But what if you are out? The best way to handle discipline when you are out is to remove your child from the situation. So if he is having a tantrum at the shopping centre, ignore him, and try to finish your shopping as quickly as possible and get out of there as fast as you can! Remember to be in tune with his signals, so don't take him shopping if he is hungry, tired or over-stimulated – it is bound to end in tears. If you need to discipline your toddler in a public place, always take him to a quiet spot around the corner so that he does not feel embarrassed.

Avoid smacking

All smacking does is teach your child that violence and aggression are appropriate and acceptable ways to gain control. Smacking also reinforces negative behaviour by giving your child attention. If you are tempted to smack, rather take a deep breath and walk away.

By setting clear limits, and using discipline appropriately, this journey (and it is a fascinating one) on which you are both travelling, will ultimately foster a sense of independence in your toddler. At the same time it will let him work out what behaviour is acceptable, for example hugging another child, and what is not, for example pulling the dog's ears.

Storms make oaks take deeper roots.

George Herbert

CHAPTER 8

Care and development 12–15 months

Emma's mom is absolutely thrilled that Emma has taken her first steps, and eagerly anticipates her first play date with her new neighbour's little one. At first Emma seems excited to have a little friend and rushes up to investigate her new playmate Jonty. In a flash, Emma has knocked him over in an effort to grab the interesting-looking toy he is holding. Jonty responds by hitting her over the head and biting her on the arm, then runs crying to his mom, who is unable to calm him down, despite offering him some ice cream. Needless to say, the afternoon is ruined, and both moms are seriously considering avoiding each other at all costs in the future. What Jonty's mom doesn't know is that Emma was merely exploring something new and interesting in her environment, and that Jonty's nervous system was already overloaded due to the fact that he had skipped his afternoon nap. He was simply overwhelmed by his environment, and when Emma knocked him over in her enthusiasm, he fell to pieces.

Sound familiar – and all too frustrating? This is typical of how one-year-olds play with each other. Their behaviour is totally unpredictable and not at all premeditated. Little toddlers at this age don't see their playmates as people with feelings at all. They are simply there as objects to play with and explore. So if they pull the dog's ears, or the tablecloth off the table, it is simply due to their need to explore their environment.

By now you have a little person on your hands. Whilst on the one hand, you may feel that your little person is 'all grown up', on the other hand she is still a baby and still needs to be treated like one. Your toddler is able to show some affection now – she will smile, laugh, babble and look for hugs. She can clap hands, and wave bye-bye.

You will be pleased to notice a sense of humour emerging – she loves to laugh and is responsive to you. Her behaviour will become very unpredictable, vacillating from very grown up behaviour such as walking and saying a few words, to collapsing in a heap in torrents of tears if a toy is taken away from her. Welcome to the world of the toddler!

SHE REMEMBERS

By the time your baby is 14 months old, she can remember meaningful events for at least eight months after they happen.

LANGUAGE DEVELOPMENT

Your little toddler has been communicating for some time now by babbling with voice intonation and emphasis. At this stage her ***receptive speech*** (what she understands) is more advanced than her ***expressive speech*** (which is what she can actually say)

By using a single word, she is able to convey the meaning of a whole sentence. So she may say the word 'dog', which may mean that she is saying, "There is the dog", "The dog is eating" or "Where is the dog"? Her vocabulary is most likely to consist of a few words (about three or four), usually the names of objects that are part of her daily life such as 'mama' or 'dada'.

She will respond to her own name, and will understand a few simple commands such as, "Where is the light?" (how clever!).

MOTOR DEVELOPMENT

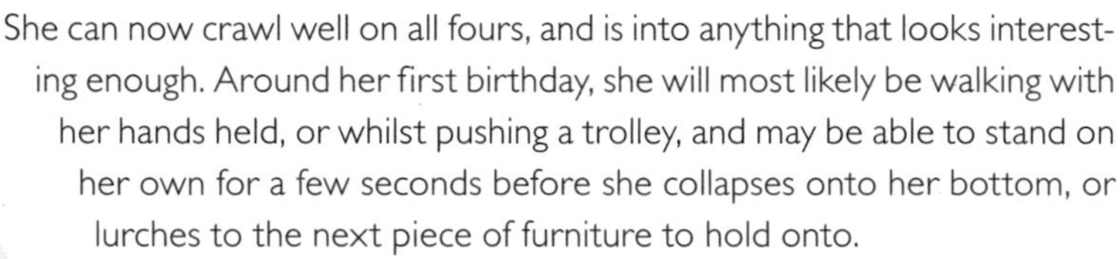

She can now crawl well on all fours, and is into anything that looks interesting enough. Around her first birthday, she will most likely be walking with her hands held, or whilst pushing a trolley, and may be able to stand on her own for a few seconds before she collapses onto her bottom, or lurches to the next piece of furniture to hold onto.

- She will be able to walk whilst holding onto furniture (cruising).
- By 15 months of age, she will most likely be walking well on her own.
- She will start to help with dressing by putting her arms up and legs into clothing.
- She will begin to be able to rise from a sitting to a standing position unaided.
- She can definitely move very quickly from her tummy or back into the sitting position, so nappy changing time can become quite challenging!
- Her grasp of large and small objects will develop fully and she will be able to hold objects with the tips of her forefingers by picking up things with a precise thumb and index finger grip (pincer grip), and will love packing and unpacking objects.

EMOTIONAL DEVELOPMENT

For anyone opportunities for emotional growth lie in every outburst of feeling. Your little toddler will experience a range of feelings when she encounters people and experiences around her. These feelings can be joy, anger, fear, curiosity or frustration. As her language skills develop, she will begin to communicate with you more effectively to express her needs. At this stage she has few words to describe how she is feeling, so she will largely communicate with you by using sounds (such as laughing or crying), and actions (see pages 31–34).

She now notices other babies around her with great interest and starts to realize that she can form a relationship (albeit very fleeting at this stage!) with them. She will stare, smile, babble away and reach out to another child in her vicinity.

Your little toddler will realize that certain ***actions*** cause certain ***reactions***. She will seek the reward of seeing you smile when she pulls a funny face.

STRATEGIES TO SELF-CALM

> As your toddler matures and grows up, she will be able to find ways to deal with her feelings and she will begin to develop strategies to self-calm after experiencing an emotional storm.

NUTRITION

Don't be alarmed if your little toddler appears to become a picky or poor eater. At this age, there is so much to explore, so many things to touch, and so many places to get to, that eating seems like a complete waste of time! You may think that because she is so active and busy, she needs more food – but this is not the case. Her growth rate slows down dramatically from one to two years. This will obviously account for some loss of appetite, and she will appear to thrive on very little other than fresh air. Children this age find it very difficult to sit still for any length of time. Little toddlers find that eating simply occupies too much sensory time, especially if they are tired, so they would rather not bother. Don't worry, this is normal.

Breastfeeding and formula milk

If you are happy to continue breastfeeding, then do so, but limit feeds to twice a day – one on waking in the morning, and the second one at bedtime in the evening. Try not to feed too close to a meal as this may spoil her appetite. If your child is healthy and thriving, you can replace formula milk with full cream, pasteurised cow's milk, unless she is allergy prone, in which case soya or goat's milk or a hypo-allergenic formula may be an option.

If your finances allow, there are many fortified toddler or growing up milks available. Try to avoid offering her formula milk as a meal replacement, "to be sure she gets her nutrition". All you will do is fill her up with milk at the risk of her losing her appetite for solid food. Milk alone is not nutritionally adequate for a child of this age.

Mixed diet

There is no special diet that small toddlers need. Most of the time they can eat what the rest of the family is eating, but remember to stick to the principle of a varied diet that includes protein such as meat, poultry, dairy, beans, nuts and seeds, carbohydrates such as bread, cereal, rice, pasta and potato and fats such as avocado, cheese and butter, as well as a variety of fruit and vegetables. Your little toddler will still enjoy slightly moist food, so it's OK to still puree her food, but do make the texture coarser. Mashing food with the back of a fork is adequate at this stage. If she is a good eater, she will most likely be having in the region of a cup (250 ml) of solid food per meal approximately three times a day, with small snacks such as fruit, yoghurt, rice cakes or biscuits in between. Don't worry though, if she prefers to eat smaller quantities more often. She will eat when she is hungry.

Offer diluted fruit juice or water throughout the day if she is thirsty. If you have not done so already, start experimenting with different tastes, like adding a little garlic, spices or onion to her food. Don't worry if she spits out or gags when you introduce something new. It is normal.

Feeding herself

She will try very hard to feed herself, and will plunge her whole fist into the bowl of food. Don't despair – this is a normal and wonderful sensory and developmental experience. Always offer finger-food at all meals and at snack time. Feeding herself finger-food helps to enhance hand-eye co-ordination, and chewing strengthens the muscles of the mouth and jaw which helps with speech development. As long as she is happy to sit in her high chair, don't be in too much of a rush to pack it away. Wait until she is older before you sit her on a chair at the table.

Supplements

It is a good idea to start your child on multivitamin syrup that has additional iron. Her intake of iron-fortified formula has either lessened or stopped altogether now. This, coupled with the fact that her eating habits are going to become rather erratic (because she is now a toddler), can lead to iron-deficiency anaemia. Iron is vital for immune function, oxygen transport in the blood and healthy functioning of the nervous system. Ask your pharmacist or clinic sister to recommend an iron supplement.

BEHAVIOUR

Even though it is becoming easier to communicate with your toddler, her language skills are still not sufficiently developed for her to communicate verbally with you. She does, however, have a powerful, inborn ability to communicate her needs, likes and dislikes to you.

Exploring her world

At this stage, your little toddler will indicate what she is feeling by her behaviour, which will be unpredictable at the best of times! This may be very trying for you, but remember that she is not deliberately disobeying you. She is simply exploring her world and what it offers her. She is also learning exactly how much power she has over you. Play and exploration is how she is going to learn about her world – so bear that in mind when she wants to put on her own shoes when you are in a hurry to get out of the house. When she persists in seemingly destructive behaviour such as drawing on the wall, remember that she doesn't know that this is destructive – she sees it rather as a way to build up her fine motor skills.

Strong feelings

Her feelings of frustration and anger are easily aroused, but are usually short-lived. She may become quite aggressive, and may lash out and bite simply out of frustration, usually owing to tiredness or hunger. Remember that it is rare at this age, for any behaviour to be pre-meditated, or due to malice. She simply does not understand that other children also have feelings.

She may pause and watch what another child does when she pulls his hair, for example (a cause and effect situation), but she certainly won't have any feelings of sympathy for him. Use these opportunities to teach her to say that she is sorry, and tell her that you do not like her behaviour. Praise her if she doesn't pull the other child's hair the next time she interacts with him. Try to make this response a habit from now on – it will be useful for many years to come.

Avoid sensory overload

As you have learntin Chapter 7, most seemingly bad behaviour in the form of tantrums is simply because your toddler may be over-stimulated and overwhelmed by her environment. So try to arrange your outings and activities to fall within her awake time, and don't try to cram too many errands into one outing. Try not to expose her to too much stimulation too quickly, especially if it is approaching her nap time.

If you have to go out and her nap time is looming, take the pram along, and let her fall asleep in the pram whilst you are out and about. Remember to take along her sleep friend (dummy, blanket or soft toy – see page 40). Should a temper tantrum occur, use the strategies discussed in on page 61.

SLEEP ISSUES

Your little toddler will most likely still be sleeping in a cot at this stage, and will not need any nutrition in the form of milk feeds during the night. Do not be in any rush to move her into a bed. She will still enjoy the feeling of security her cot affords her. If the cot is big enough, she may be quite comfortable in it until at least her second birthday. In the early part of her second year, she is more of a baby than a toddler, and still needs plenty of sleep.

Set the stage for healthy sleep habits

Setting the stage for healthy sleep habits is important, so remember to watch her awake time between sleeps during the day (3–3½ hrs), and to use calming stimuli when the sleep time is due, by keeping her environment calm. At bedtime, which must not be too late, a warm bath, a massage and deep hugs all contribute towards calming. Sticking to a routine is still very important to avoid overtiredness and over-stimulation (see page 40).

Sleep training

When sleep deprivation caused by delayed bed times and night wakings affects your health and well being to the extent that your role as care-giver becomes compromised, or is making your toddler very irritable during the day, sleep training may well be the best option. The first step is to satisfy any basic needs and address any medical problems that may prevent your toddler from having healthy sleep habits (see page 38). There may be times when your toddler will cry and protest the breaking of old habits, while you are teaching her to sleep through the night. By following these simple guidelines, your child will go to sleep without resistance, will be happier with her world during the day, and you will feel stronger and more able to deal with ***your*** sensory environment!

GETTING THE NIGHTS RIGHT

You will have to teach your little toddler that she **is** able to go to sleep **on her own**. She may be used to you rocking or feeding her to sleep, or she may be used to your presence in the room before she will settle. She needs to learn ***self-soothing strategies*** such as sucking her fingers or a dummy, stroking her face or hair, or holding a security object like a soft toy or a comfort blanket. Don't give her a bottle of milk or juice as a self-soothing strategy – this will only lead to a bad habit that is hard to break.

Controlled crying works very well in these instances. As long as you know that her basic physical and emotional needs are being met, this will have no adverse effect on her. There are many differing opinions on how to handle controlled crying, but by following the simple guidelines below, your small toddler will learn to self-calm and put herself to sleep, but most importantly, will know that you are *always* there for her, and that she actually does not need to cry any more to get your attention.

- Ensure that the stage is set for sleep.
- Check whether she has any basic needs or illness to be taken care of.
- Give her a chance to settle independently by letting her fuss for up to five minutes. Note that this is not full-blown crying, but rather tired moaning just before she falls asleep.
- Limit the amount of time you spend rocking, holding or singing to her before bedtime.

LEAVING YOUR TODDLER

If your toddler begins to cry the minute you leave her side, meet her emotional needs immediately by going back to her to reassure her – try not to pick her up. Rather stand next to her cot, say something reassuring, and gently stroke or pat her back until she is calm. Always re-enforce her sleep association by tucking her teddy or blanket back under her arm and say, "Here is teddy. He needs to go to sleep now". If she is very upset, it is quite OK to pick her up and hold her until she is calm.

- If you are trying to break a feeding-to-sleep habit, pick her up if she does not settle, and gently rock her until she falls asleep, no matter how much she protests. Only place her back into her cot when she is asleep. Repeat this each time she wakes. It may take a few sessions (maybe a day or two) for her to learn that she doesn't need to feed in order to fall asleep. Move to the next step when you are ready.
- If you are trying to break a rocking-to-sleep habit, pick her up and hold her close until she stops crying. As soon as she is calm and drowsy, *but not asleep,* place her gently back into her cot. Say some soothing words and walk away from the cot, even if she begins to protest.
- Stay away from her for *one minute*, then return to her side if she is still protesting.
- Pick her up and settle her (no matter how long it takes). Reinforce the sleep object. When she is calm and drowsy, *but not asleep,* place her gently back into her cot.
- This time, wait for *two minutes* before going back to her if she is still crying, then repeat your calming strategies.
- If necessary, repeat the procedure, each time *adding two minutes* of crying time before going back in to soothe or settle her.
- Keep going each time she wakes in the night, starting from *one minute* of separation at the start of each session.

STAYING WITH YOUR TODDLER

If you would rather stay with your little toddler, sit with her and put a hand on her, keeping her in the lying down position (not an easy task with a wriggly toddler). Let her snuggle down with her sleep object.

- Don't move your hand, and don't talk, except to say, "Ssshhh" quietly and repeatedly. She may wriggle and cry for a while – it will seem like an eternity. If she stands up, despite your hand on her back, place her back into the lying down position and re-offer the sleep object. Do this each time she wakes on the first night.
- The next night (or whenever you are ready), sit next to her and don't touch her. If she stands up, place her back into the lying down position. Reinforce her sleep object. Still soothe her with your voice and your presence, no matter how much she protests.
- The following night (or whenever you are ready), move further from the cot so that she can feel your presence and hear your voice and be soothed by this. If she stands up, place her back into the lying down position, and reinforce the sleep object.
- Each subsequent night (or as you progress at your own pace), move further away from the cot, but remain in the room. Each time she stands up, place her back into the lying down position, and re-enforce her sleep object.

- Within a week (or longer if you have paced it out), you should be able to leave the room.

HAVE REALISTIC EXPECTATIONS

With both methods, expect your toddler to have more periods of unsettledness than actual sleep for the first few sessions, perhaps even for a night or two.

- Be prepared for her nights to get worse before they improve, but persevere.
- Expect a protest or revenge night approximately a week down the line, when she will again cry for longer and will need your presence in the room once more. Handle this revenge night in a calm and consistent manner, and it will soon pass.
- Be loving and giving, but remain firm and consistent.
- Spend some extra time during the day playing and cuddling with her. It will do you both the world of good.

OTHER ISSUES

The most important gift that you can give your toddler is emotional intelligence, which is a strong sense of self, through your unconditional love and acceptance of who she is.

Play

As a parent of an increasingly mobile toddler whose desire to explore her world seems insatiable, your role in enriching her experiences by attributing meaning to them is unique. Try to be a parent first and foremost, and avoid adopting a teacher role as you feel pressured by society to stimulate your child and teach her skills to enable her to cope with the demands of school, and indeed the 21st century. Children are designed to learn through play. Allocating special playtime with your toddler is an investment in your future together.

A specific way of playing with toddlers called a "Child-centred approach" was developed by Dr Stanley Greenspan (MD) in 1998. This involves a daily session of 15–20 minutes of uninterrupted play between you and your child, in a focussed and non-judgemental manner. This special time is unrushed, and you need to be in close proximity on the floor. Allow your toddler to initiate play, and all you have to do is 'watch, wait and wonder' and enter into your child's world. Admire, imitate and develop her activity and play theme, but avoid praising her. Say, "What a lovely doll! I agree that she looks beautiful!", rather than, "What a good girl you are for dressing your doll so beautifully".

Remember that this is fun time, not teaching time, so ensure that the environment is both toddler-proof and rich in sensory stimulation in the form of textured and moving toys, as well as typical toys like dolls and cars. Structured toys such as puzzles are to be avoided as they dampen your toddler's sense of exploration. Anything that your toddler chooses to do is acceptable, provided she is not hurting herself (or you), or destroying her toys. This type of play fosters emotional growth in the enjoyment of exploring and doing things together. When the allocated time is up, tidy up together and move on to another activity such as having a snack or reading a story.

FLEXIBLE ROUTINE

- Your little toddler should now be eating solids from all food groups spread between breakfast, lunch and supper with small snacks mid-morning and afternoon, or she may prefer to eat five small meals a day.
- She will need approximately 500 ml of milk a day, given on waking and at bedtime.
- Your little toddler will sleep for approximately 10–12 hours a night without needing milk or any nutrition.
- Limit her awake time to 3–3 ½ hours between sleeps and plan your care giving, outings and stimulation within this time.
- She will still be having two sleeps a day, varying from 45 minutes to 2 hours in length (in total approximately 3 hours).
- She should be sleeping 14–15 hours in a 24 hour cycle.

ACTIVITIES AND TOYS TO ENHANCE DEVELOPMENT

Helping your little toddler channel her spontaneous but potentially destructive exuberance in a safe way will always be a challenge! Outdoor play should be encouraged as running, bouncing and climbing help to develop *co-ordination and body awareness.* Swinging her upside down and rocking her on a rocking horse help to develop her sense of *movement* and will improve her balance and co-ordination.

Your little toddler will enjoy repeating activities over and over again, particularly those that involve packing and unpacking, removing and replacing lids or sorting nesting bowls. These repeated activities help her to refine her *fine motor and sorting skills* and as she improves, will provide her with a tremendous sense of achievement. She will often hold a toy or object close to her eyes as she studies it before deciding what to do with it. This is how her *visual perception* develops.

To stimulate her *language skills* and *auditory perception*, talk to her all the time as you go about your daily activities, pose questions to her and expose her to a variety of sounds ranging from classical music to jangly nursery rhymes.

To stimulate her sense of *taste and smell*, start introducing new flavours into her diet. Have fun with her by teaching her to sniff new and interesting smells such as scented toys and flowers with perfume. Playing with vegetables provides real experience with texture, smell, form and taste. She will still explore with her mouth and will love to eat the sand in her sandpit, as well as anything else

that interests her. Don't be too paranoid about what she tastes, as long as it's not toxic!

Expose her skin to new and different ***touch*** sensations by tickling her with various objects such as a feather or soft hair brush, and let her help you rub cream into her body after a bath. Unless it is very cold, or the surface is dangerous, allow her to walk barefoot.

If a toy rolls away from her, encourage her to go after it and find it herself – this will help develop her ***spatial perception***. Invest in a swing made from a rubber tyre and hang it from a tree in your garden, or take her to the park – swinging will help develop her sense of movement.

See Chapter 3 pages 28–30 for more ideas to either calm or stimulate her **sensory system**.

WATER PLAY

Your toddler will be fascinated with water. In summer, let a trickle of water come out of the hosepipe and let her play outside with it on the lawn (unless you have water restrictions). Put some water in a small paddle pool (cover the bottom with about 2 inches of water). Let your little toddler sit in the pool and play with a variety of empty containers and plastic toys. Teach her how to blow bubbles in the water. This will help develop the muscles of her mouth to aid speech development. **Always supervise water play.**

When it rains, go and jump in the puddles together.

Ideas for toys and equipment

- building blocks and simple construction toys
- giant pegboard and hammer
- paddle pool
- sandpit and accessories
- snap or click together toys
- ball pond
- toy telephone on wheels or any pull-along toy
- canisters of different sizes
- music tapes or compact discs
- swing
- cardboard box
- ride-on car
- rocking horse

These are some simple ideas to have fun with your little toddler whilst at the same time enhancing her development. For more in-depth stimulation ideas read all or any of these books:

- *Clever talk* by Martie Pieterse (Metz Press. 1999)
- *School readiness through play* by Martie Pieterse (Metz Press. 2001)
- *Brain gym for all* by Melodie de Jager (Human & Rosseau. 2001)
- *Entertaining and educating babies and toddlers* by Roby Gee and Susan Meredith (Usborne. 1986)

SENSE-ABLE SECRET
Remember that quiet time is also important, so don't go overboard with stimulation.

TEETH

By one year of age, your toddler should have four top teeth and four bottom teeth. At around 14 months of age, the first molars begin to appear. Some children teethe later, and only get their first teeth at this stage, and molars at around 18 months of age, so don't worry if your toddler is taking her time! Make teeth brushing a part of your daily routine.

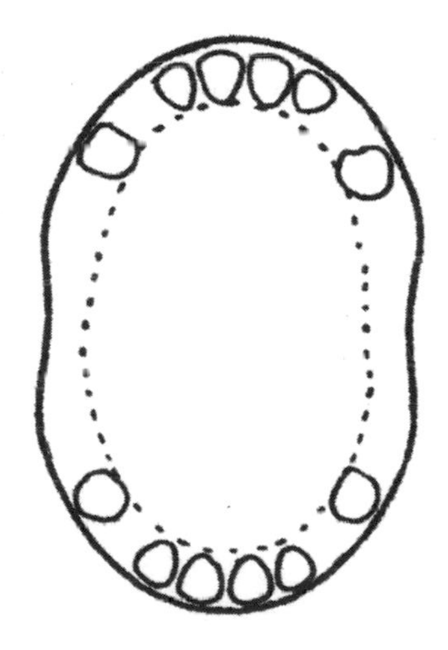

Care of your toddler's teeth

Now that your little one has teeth, it is important that you start including dental hygiene in your daily routine. The easiest way to do this is to show your child, by example, how to brush her teeth with a toothbrush. A good idea is to give her an age-appropriate sized toothbrush when she is in the bath, and introduce it as a fun thing to do. As she gets older, you can incorporate brushing teeth into the bedtime routine, so that going to the toilet, washing hands, then brushing teeth are all part of going to bed. When she is older, the same can apply to a 'going to school' routine – toilet, wash hands, brush teeth, then leave for school. The taste of adult toothpaste may be too strong for your child to start with, so use baby toothpaste for the first few years.

Dental visits should start with accompanying you when you visit the dentist. She can get to know your dentist in a friendly and unthreatening way, and have a bit of fun riding on the chair to start with. As she becomes familiar with the environment (and gets more teeth), it will become easier for the dentist to look at her teeth. You don't want your toddler to be around should you need serious dental work, so enlist some help for these visits, so that your child can be taken out the room after the fun bits! It is a good idea to visit your dentist every 6 months.

CPR AND FIRST AID

Your little tot will most likely be walking by now and will be more inquisitive than ever. Check your home environment carefully to make sure that your swimming pool, fountains and ponds are securely netted and fenced off, and that all poisonous and harmful objects and substances are safely locked away. This is an ideal time to update your CPR and first aid knowledge (don't forget to include your nanny and your domestic worker), and stock up your first aid kit. For details of first aid and CPR classes in your area, contact the Child Accident Prevention Foundation of South Africa,at tel. 011 792 4332 or 021 685 5208 or www.altonsa.co.za/childsafe.

It isn't the big pleasures that count the most;
it's making a great deal out of the little ones.

JEAN WEBSTER

CHAPTER 9

Care and development 15-18 months

Michael is now 17 months old and loves being outside, especially if he has a ball in his hands. He has become bored with his big ball that was easy to roll and throw, and now his dad is teaching him to throw and kick a smaller ball. He is trying very hard to do this without falling over, but he is getting better at it each time he tries. His dad, of course, is already planning Michael's international soccer career and loves spending time outdoors with him. Michael is very attached to his ball, especially if his cousin shows interest in it, in which case Michael snatches it away from him and shouts a vehement "NO".

Your little toddler has progressed to a not so little toddler! He is a sociable little boy now and is starting to show interest in other children in his environment. He is also at the stage where he will challenge the limits of safety by testing whether he can touch the electrical plug, or unbuckle his seat belt while riding in the car. Michael has not yet learned to share, or have any understanding of the needs of anyone else other than himself, as he still does not know that any other people exist separately from himself. Michael is able to point to objects that he is interested in, and will be trying desperately to process speech and language to some degree. Michael has also learned that there are two sides to his body, divided down the middle, and that he has two of the same body parts on either side (for example two arms, two legs). He has also realized that he has only one of each part that is positioned in the midline (for example one nose, one bellybutton). He's growing up!

LANGUAGE DEVELOPMENT

By now Michael should know where to localise a sound source and to discriminate between different voices, and to understand different tones (happy, cross). He will be able to respond to his name, and will come when you call him. Bear in mind that his **receptive speech** (what he understands) is far more advanced than his **expressive speech** (what he can actually say), so you may not always understand what he is trying to say. However, it is at this stage that he will start to learn his first real words. These are different words to his first gobbledegook baby words. You will be amazed at how quickly his language development takes place, and by the time Michael is 18 months old he may have a vocabulary of about 20 or more words, and may even use two or three words together.

CHECKLIST FOR HEARING

- He reacts to loud noises.
- He is able to imitate sounds.
- He responds to his name.

MOTOR DEVELOPMENT

Your toddler should be able to stand and walk completely by himself by now, even though it may be on tip-toe at times. He is definitely becoming more agile and is starting to climb. He will love being outdoors and can now master the art of rolling and catching a large ball (how clever!). He may also be able to throw and kick a small ball without falling over and will take great delight in doing it over and over again. Be sure to praise him – it is a big achievement for him. He should be able to recognise and point to body parts and learn what they are used for, so encourage him to show you his tummy, eyes and so on. He knows too, that his arms and legs can function on their own, but if they work together he is able to perform more co-ordinated movements. Your toddler is moving and shaking!

His fine-motor development is also coming along, and he will love to scribble on any surface that is available. He is definitely becoming more dextrous and will handle play dough with ease and will attempt to do up his buttons.

EMOTIONAL DEVELOPMENT

He will become quite clingy and possessive at this stage ("Mine!") and will exasperate you as his emotions vacillate from happy to miserable at the drop of a hat.

However, his self-esteem is growing as he slowly begins to master his environment, which will help him to become less frustrated and insecure. This is also helped by the fact that his language skills are developing, so communication is becoming easier, although he will still use sounds and actions to express most of his needs.

Help him make sense of his feelings

This magic thread of communication enables him to keep in emotional contact with you. It is important, that *you*, as the parent help to *make sense* of any feelings your toddler may be feeling. It is unreasonable at this stage to expect him to be left alone to make sense of his feelings. The first step is to *acknowledge* the feeling, then give it a *name*. So when your child bursts into tears because the dog barked loudly, you could say to him, " I know that you are frightened of the dog, but it's OK." This way, you give him a message that whatever he is feeling or experiencing is manageable and not out of control. These strategies, as well as non-verbal cues such as smiles and nods, will also reassure him.

It is amazing to think that many of life's important messages are learnt during this stage, for example love and approval as opposed to hate and rejection. Allow him to use facial expressions to reflect his moods without admonishing him. After all, this is how he tells you about his state (see page 32).

If he is upset, his lip will quiver, he will have downcast eyes, with a furrowed brow, clenched fists and a jutting jaw. These signs will also show you that he is avoiding contact. If so, help him with some self-calming strategies such as allowing him to retreat to a place where he feels safe and secure such as his special sensory place (see below).

If he is feeling happy and mischievous, he will invite interaction with you or others with giggling and sparkling eyes (see sensory signals page 32). Allow him the space and freedom to explore and develop his unique personality traits.

Special sensory place

Try to create a special sensory place in your home where your toddler can go when he is feeling overwhelmed (sensory overload). A small tent filled with pillows in the corner of his bedroom, or a big puffy beanbag or favourite blanket provides a special place for him to have some quiet time to 'regroup' in a safe environment. This is a useful place for him to go to when he has been sent to his room for time out (see page 64). Encourage calming activities (see table on pages 28–30) to help regulate his emotions as well as his sensory system.

BECOMING A BIG BOY

By the age of 18 months, your toddler's birth weight has almost tripled and his height has definitely doubled.

NUTRITION

By now your little munchkin is asserting his independence in wanting to feed himself with a spoon or fork, and wants to drink from a cup unaided. Show him how to use his fork to spear food – he will be very pleased with himself when he manages this! Allow him to feed himself, despite the mess – it is good for him!

Be relaxed about mealtimes

Try not to turn mealtimes into a monumental battle with your toddler. Offer him two choices per meal, and let him eat what he wants. The more you push him to eat, the less likely he is to do so. He will pick up on your anxiety and play up, so try to be relaxed about mealtimes. He will most likely be losing interest in his early morning milk, so you can drop this feed if necessary. His milk needs are in the region of 500–600 ml per day, made up of one or two milk feeds, cheese and yoghurt, or for use in cooking. If you are happy to continue to breastfeed, then do so, but limit breastfeeds to twice a day. Iron-fortified toddler milks are great, but if finances are a problem, full cream cow's milk will do. If your child is allergy prone or has a history of dairy intolerance, it may be advisable to keep him on a hypo-allergenic milk until two years of age. Don't fall into the trap of offering him milk feeds instead of solid food.

Some toddlers this age appear to have no appetite, and seem to exist on very little food. Don't stress – he will eat when he is hungry.

Keep the balance

Make sure his diet includes at least three servings (1 serving = 1 heaped tablespoon) of protein such as meat, dairy, poultry, nuts, beans or eggs per day, as well as a variety of fruit and vegetables. If he hates vegetables don't fret unduly; offer vegetable juice or disguise vegetables with minced meat, pasta, or quiche (see recipes, Appendix D, page 137). Similarly, if he hates fruit, make ice lollies, jelly or smoothies with fresh fruit juice.

Try to avoid fruit and vegetable juice that has added sugar, artificial flavourants and colourants, as these can cause allergies and hyperactivity.

He may begin to lose interest in pureed food, and will prefer his food chopped into small pieces. If he is still enjoying pureed food, make the texture coarser (mashing with the back of a fork will do) and offer him finger food at each meal.

If your child is healthy and thriving, don't worry too much about what you may think is a varied and tasty diet. You will drive yourself crazy trying to be imaginative about menus and meals.

HEALTHY TREATS

As a rule of thumb, try to keep sweets and junk food to an absolute minimum, and don't use them only on a reward basis. Offer a juicy piece of fruit, or a few raisins, or a date ball (see recipes) as a special treat.

Let him choose

Offer your toddler what you know he likes, as long as it is not junk food. So, if he loves macaroni and cheese, give it to him twice a day if needs be. You could try sneaking in a bit of tomato, some cold meat or beans and see what his reaction is. He will soon be off the macaroni and develop a passion for meat balls and gravy! Let him guide you as to how much he wants to eat. Toddlers have days (just like us) when they are more, or less hungry than usual.

Suggested menu

(This is purely a guideline to give you an idea of meals.)

Milk (breastmilk, cow's milk or formula) on waking – as much as he likes provided it does not take away his breakfast appetite. He may prefer a few sips of water or tea.

Breakfast	Boiled egg Small piece of fruit ½ slice of brown toast 100 ml of fruit juice or milk
Mid-morning snack	Water or diluted fruit juice Handful of raisins
Lunch	Cheese sandwich made with 1 slice of brown bread Small yoghurt and/or 100 ml milk
Mid-afternoon snack	2 thin cucumber slices Small piece of fruit Small biscuit
Dinner	1–2 Meat balls Tablespoon of brown rice and gravy Teaspoon of peas One baby carrot Finger of zucchini
After supper/bedtime	As much milk as he prefers, either breast, formula or cow's milk.

BEHAVIOUR

This is the age where your toddler may be determined to do things for himself. He may become quite aggressive, hitting or biting his playmates. It is difficult for you as a parent or caregiver to control his behaviour every moment of the day, so when he scribbles on the walls, he doesn't know that he is destroying the paintwork, he is simply enjoying his new-found fine motor-skills! And when he refuses to go to bed, it's only because he finds that being with you is so exciting, and bedtime is so boring! At this age, he acts on nearly every impulse, so these seemingly defiant and destructive behaviours are quite normal. It will take time for him to develop the self-control to behave appropriately, so the good news is that he will, with time, grow out of the destructive behaviours. Allow him to start to develop his own will, but be firm, loving and consistent when some discipline is needed. However, if your child hits, bites or lashes out inappropriately, or picks up other nasty habits, then it is your job to take control *for* him, by helping him develop the self-discipline he needs to express his emotions in safer ways (see page 62).

SLEEP ISSUES

There may be many reasons for the fact that your little toddler suddenly feels apprehensive about going to bed. He may not want to go to bed alone, or he may wake up frequently during the night, needing either your presence or a bottle to go back to sleep. When delayed bedtimes and night wakings are beginning to impact on your ability to parent effectively, or your relationships are suffering, then it may be time to consider some sleep training. As your toddler will most likely still be sleeping in a cot, this is a good time to start, as it is a lot harder to teach a child to sleep on his own when he is able to get out of bed on his own!

He may be teething, so if this is the case, speak to your clinic sister or pharmacist about teething remedies. The first step is to make sure that your little toddler is not ill, so a full medical check-up is advised. Once he has a clean bill of health, you can adopt the strategies as discussed in Chapter 8 (see pages 72–74). Remember the importance of routine (see page 40), and early to bed as well as using the following sensory calming strategies:

- Watching awake times (see page 40);
- Removing him from a noisy and overly visually stimulating environment;
- Giving him a warm bath;
- Deep-pressure massage and cuddles after his bath;
- Singing lullabyes;
- Letting him suck – either milk or breast – before bedtime (night) or non-nutritive sucking on his fingers or a dummy;
- Sleep associations such as soft toy or cuddle blanket.

OTHER ISSUES

Even the nicest toddlers can develop some nasty habits, so don't be unduly worried if your little one picks up the odd habit. Some of these may only appear when your toddler is a little older, but I discuss them all here for ease of reference.

By following these simple guidelines to get rid of them, they should be a transient and temporary state of events, and should cause no lasting harm.

Aggression

As awful as it may be to you, aggression is a normal part of toddler development. Language skills that are not fully developed yet, coupled with a fierce desire to become independent, as well as difficulties with impulse-control can cause your toddler to become quite aggressive at times. Hitting, throwing, biting and hair pulling can be classed as aggressive behaviour. Try to show him other ways to express his feelings of anger and frustration (like hitting a punch bag or pillow). Being in tune with your child's sensory signals (see pages 28–30 00), will help you to pre-empt aggressive behaviour, giving you time to step in before the behaviour gets out of hand. Children often do nasty things if they are feeling tired, hungry and overloaded.

Biting

Biting is a fairly common behaviour in small toddlers. It can be a normal part of development when verbal skills are not fully developed, and should stop at around the age of three. It is not pre-meditated or hateful, it is rather an 'acting out' of great feelings of frustration and anger. No matter how tempted you are to shout, smack or even bite back, the best way to handle the situation is to ignore the perpetrator (the one that bites) and shower all the attention on the victim.

Show your child that you are displeased by the tone of your voice and your body language (turn your back on him), and turn all your attention to the child he has bitten. If your child is old enough, you can use time out (see page 64). When it is all over, talk the situation through with your child. Even if your child does not have many verbal skills, it is still important to do this because it will show him that talking (not biting) is the way to solve problems. Some children bite because their sensory system is overloaded. Try implementing calming strategies as discussed on page 61.

Hitting

Some children hit or lash out at others for much the same reasons as biting. Handle hitting episodes the same as you would biting.

Hair pulling

When your toddler pulls on the hair of his playmate, it is most likely because he is feeling frustrated at his dismal attempts of verbalising how he is feeling. As with biting or hitting, it is not pre-meditated or hateful. Handle it in the same way as you would biting and hitting.

Throwing

Throwing things is a new and enjoyable skill for many toddlers. He has discovered that whatever he throws will fall down – he's discovering gravity! Try to ignore aggressive throwing if possible (remember, if you respond, he is likely to do it again). However, there may come a point when you will have to discourage aggressive throwing by saying to him, "We don't throw sand in our sister's eyes because it can hurt her". Remember to give extra attention to the 'victim'. Rather show him what he *can* throw by saying, "Balls are for throwing outside, but sand isn't.

Nose picking

Most toddlers pick their noses when they have nothing better to do! Some toddlers find great comfort from delving into their nostrils and use it as a way of self-calming (see page 33). Sometimes an older toddler picks his nose purely to annoy his parents!

Either way, apart from being in tune with his signals and pre-empting the behaviour and distracting him, try your best to ignore it.

Nail biting

Nail biting can be a result of many factors. Your toddler may simply be bored, or curious as to what nails taste like. Often though, nail biting can be due to anxiety as he faces the daily challenges of growing up. If you notice that your toddler bites his nails on those occasions (such as the first day at playschool, or meeting strangers), don't worry.

This is simply his way of coping with a bit of stress and of self-calming. Offer him plenty of reassurance about the 'trigger' situation and avoid nagging or punishing him.

Lying

Toddlers seldom deliberately try to conceal or distort the truth. At this age your toddler is not generally able to tell right from wrong, and bear in mind that he is still learning to distinguish fantasy from reality. Later on, your four year old may tell you something that he wants you to hear, for instance he may tell you that he has put his cup in the sink when in fact he hasn't, because he knows that you will be pleased to hear this. Try not to overreact when he tells the odd lie, as he isn't lying in the true sense of the word. As he gets older, you can start teaching him that it is wrong to say something that is not true, but for now, don't worry too much.

Masturbation

Toddlers discover their private parts when the nappy area is unveiled and a new area of discovery is made available. Remember that body exploration is all part of growing up. They may touch or rub their genitalia, and may move their legs or rock their bodies purely for the pleasurable feeling, especially if their emotional or sensory system is overwhelmed. Masturbation generally occurs when your toddler is tired, bored or anxious, so be in tune with those sensory signals (see page 33), and distract and divert his attention elsewhere. Never smack or humiliate him when he is masturbating; it is an innocent habit and if ignored, will soon pass.

Head banging

Surprisingly enough head banging is fairly common. It can occur during a tantrum in the young toddler, but can also be used as a way of sensory calming when your toddler is feeling overwhelmed by his environment, or when he is over-tired. Some toddlers bang their heads when they are bored, and use it as a mild form of entertainment! Be in tune with your toddler's sensory signals (see page 33) and avoid over-tiredness and sensory overload by watching awake times (see page 40).

Head banging is not a sign of bad behaviour but can be a pleasurable event for your child, so relax – most children outgrow this habit by the time they are 2½ years old. If your child is older than three years, and still likes to bang his head and if you are worried about other behavioural or developmental issues, it is advisable to seek professional medical advice as there may be neurological reasons(see Appendices A and B).

SENSE-ABLE SECRET

Your toddler's emotions will be unregulated at this stage. When he feels out of control and emotionally overwhelmed, help him to calm down by holding him firmly against your body (try holding a pillow behind him for a deeper hug) and applying pressure on his head with your hand.

FLEXIBLE ROUTINE

- Your toddler should be eating solids from all food groups spread between breakfast, lunch and supper, with small snacks mid morning and afternoon.
- He may prefer to eat five small meals a day, rather than three large meals with small snacks.
- He may drop his early morning milk, and prefer water, or tea at this time. He may prefer to have only one bottle of milk (or a breastfeed) per day, usually at bedtime.
- Bedtime is between 6 and 7 pm depending on the last sleep of the afternoon
- Your toddler will sleep for 11–12 hours at night without needing any milk feeds.
- Limit his awake time to 3–4 hours between sleeps and plan your care-giving, outings and stimulation within this time.
- He may still need two sleeps a day, varying from 45 minutes to 2 hours.
- He should be sleeping for 13–15 hours in a 24 hour cycle.

ACTIVITIES AND TOYS TO ENHANCE DEVELOPMENT

At this age (and, in fact, for a while to come), your toddler has an inner drive to be part of what is happening around him. Use every opportunity to stimulate him in a way that is balanced and beneficial.

As we know, from a sensory perspective, ***auditory*** stimulation is very important from an early age, but more so now, as his language skills are developing. Listening skills need to be enhanced as these provide the foundation on which your child's speech and language abilities and literacy skills are built. Talk to your toddler all the time, telling him about what you are doing: "I'm filling up the kettle with water and turning it on …". Play different types of sounds and music to teach him the difference between tone and pitch. To enhance his listening skills, give him simple instructions such as, "Please fetch Mommy's handbag". Be sure to praise him when he gets it right.

Sequencing is an understanding of what comes first, as well as the ability to visually place objects, pictures or shapes in a sequence or logical pattern. By showing him that socks come before shoes, you will teach him that all daily activities have a sequence.

Clown around and let him copy you dancing and jumping. You will be amazed at how much he will learn simply through imitation, so let him copy you making funny faces, blowing bubbles, sticking out your tongue and playing peek a boo – this aids his *visual* development.

Encourage *outdoor play.* Rolling, jumping, swimming with water wings, swinging and spinning are all good exercises for developing *body awareness and co-ordination.* Ride-on toys are great for improving his balance and spatial awareness. How he will love that feeling of independence and mobility!

For *fine motor-skills*, get his little fingers kneading and rolling play dough, and show him how to use his thumb and index finger to achieve more complex tasks like doing up buttons and threading. Shape sorters will help him to develop an awareness of different shapes and will help with fine motor skills. He will still love to do any repetitive task such as packing and unpacking objects into canisters, taking lids off and putting them back on, and filling and spilling containers with water. Fill a bowl with soapy water and give him a sponge and some small plastic plates. **Always** supervise water play.

Let him *touch, taste* and *sniff* new and different textures, food and smells. Let him walk barefoot, unless it is very cold.

See Chapter 3, page 28–30 for suggestions on calming or stimulating your toddler's **sensory system**

Ideas for toys and equipment

- jungle gym
- trampoline
- swing
- stable ride-on toys (with four wheels)
- paddle pool
- balls
- shape sorters
- pegboard with hammer
- building blocks and simple construction toys
- threading toys
- tea set
- miniature broom and mop (for both girls and boys!)
- music tapes or compact discs
- pull-along toys
- play dough (see recipe Appendix D)

- bubbles
- finger and roller paints
- board books

For more in-depth stimulation ideas use these books:
- *Clever talk* by Martie Pieterse (Metz Press. 1999)
- *School readiness through play* by Martie Pieterse (Metz Press. 2001)
- *Brain gym for all* by Melodie de Jager (Human & Rosseau. 2001)
- *Entertaining and educating babies and toddlers* by Roby Gee and Susan Meredith (Usborne. 1986)

BUILDING SKILLS

Bear in mind that each new skill your child develops stems from an existing, less organised skill, so follow his cues as he learns, trust your instinct and he will reward you with many hours of pleasure and fun.

MORE TEETH

He may only be cutting his first molars (top and bottom) now. If he already has them, this is the time that the cuspids (between the molars and the incisors) on both top and bottom will start to appear.

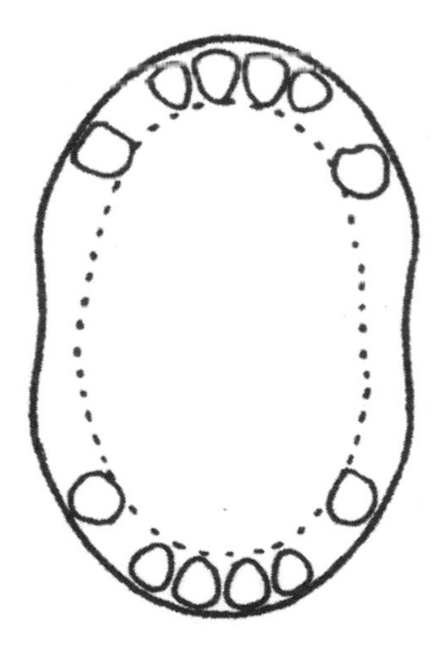

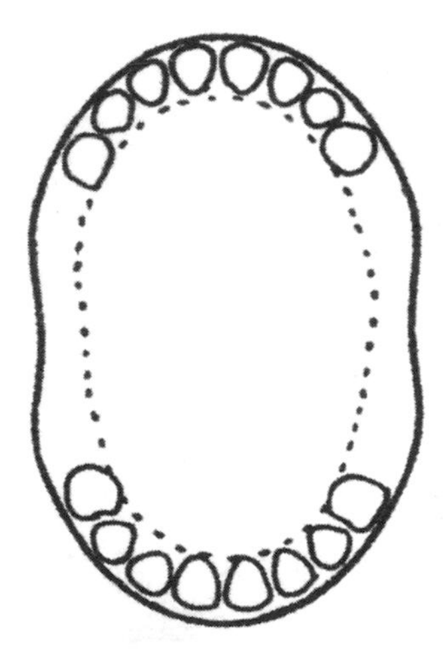

TODDLER WORKSHOPS

If you haven't been attending baby stimulation or music classes, consider enrolling your toddler in a toddler workshop of the same nature. These classes are a great opportunity for your toddler to learn to socialise with other tots the same age, whilst having fun. They also offer the opportunity for you to make some new friends who have children the same age as yours.

Teach us to delight in simple things.

Rudyard Kipling

CHAPTER 10

Care and development 18–24 months

Alison has just turned 20 months. She is warm and loving when she feels like it, but seems to have become a bit clingy and weepy of late. Her parents, John and Anne-Marie are concerned, as they don't want Alison to be shy and unfriendly, but are unsure how to handle these moody periods. When Alison is in a good mood, she hardly notices them and plays and runs around fearlessly causing many anxious moments for her parents as she scoots to the very top of the jungle gym, or runs away from them in a flash. Anne-Marie can't remember when last she was able to have a hot cup of tea or talk on the telephone without interruption!

This is often the most challenging and rewarding time of parenting! Your little toddler can now walk steadily on her own, has started to run, climb and jump. Mother Nature has been at work, and has made sure that the last fontanelle (opening on the skull) has now closed. This means that your toddler's skull is now a most effective crash helmet so that when she has her tumbles, her brain is protected from harm.

The days of being able to place your little one on an activity mat within a circle of toys and expect her to quietly amuse herself are long gone! She is learning to identify objects from visual stimuli (sight), and is able to understand most simple instructions. (How clever she is !)

She will start to really love singing and dancing, and will try to join in with words and actions.

LANGUAGE DEVELOPMENT

Your toddler will definitely respond to her name by now, and may even refer to herself by her name, for example *"Ally mine"*. She will start to imitate simple words and will have a vocabulary of 20–50 words, reaching about 50–100 as she gets closer to two years of age. She may even manage to use two to three words together such as, *"Go away"*. She should be able to identify simple pictures when you name them. For example, if you asked her, ***"Show me the teddy in the picture"*** she would proudly oblige. She will love to do simple movements to songs that she recognises.

It is important to note that the first two years of life are a critical period for learning ***language,*** and your child should have developed some auditory processing skills by now. By the age of two years, she should be able to localise a sound source as well as discriminate between different voices and sounds (for example mom's voice as opposed to the dog barking).

Bear in mind that all toddlers develop at their own pace, so if your child still gestures more than speaks at this stage, but has a clear understanding of what you are saying, don't worry.

This is the time when she starts classifying and grouping objects, and anything round may be called 'ball'. She will love to imitate the sound of things and animals. Encourage her, and make her aware of the sounds around her, from the bird song early in the morning to the sound of the cars passing in the street. Talk to her when you do everyday routine things so that she will ***hear*** words used in simple sentence constructions while ***seeing*** or ***touching*** the objects referred to. Involve as many senses as possible in your interaction with her to enhance her development.

This is the time of many questions. Follow her cue and ask her questions to encourage her to use her new-found language skills.

MOTOR DEVELOPMENT

Your toddler should now be able to walk all on her own, even negotiating steps, as well as manage to walk backwards. She will want to walk down steps forwards as long as she has something to hold onto for balance, but if she feels unsure, will crawl down stairs backwards. Her ***sense of balance*** is maturing – she may be able to balance (momentarily) on one foot, and often plays crouching on her haunches. She will be able to confidently throw a small ball without falling over, and may even be able to kick with one foot, using her other leg for balance.

She will be able to ***carry*** lightweight and smallish objects, so she can start to help you around the house by taking her bowl to the kitchen, and will be able to ***bend over*** and pick up her toys without falling over. This ability to carry small objects will come in very handy for when any siblings arrive!

Her ***pincer grip*** (between the tip of her thumb and index finger) is now mature, so she will be able to pick up small things and manipulate them as she likes, such as turning the pages of a book, scribbling with a crayon, or placing small objects one on top of the other. Watch out for small objects such as buttons, seed pods and beads – she can still choke on these, as well as stick them into any possible opening!

She now has the ***wrist mobility*** to keep food on a spoon to feed herself (relatively) successfully (be prepared for plenty of mess), and will try very hard to brush her own hair and teeth.

She will get great pleasure from co-operating with dressing activities, and will exasperate you by removing items of her clothing, particularly socks, shoes and hats, especially when you are in a hurry!

EMOTIONAL DEVELOPMENT

Alison is now realizing that her parents and herself are ***not*** one and the same person (up until now she thought they were). She is starting to develop a sense of herself as a separate body and mind. Having always received plenty of security and acknowledgement from her parents, Alison has started to make this important distinction and will start to develop her own individual character traits. This realization can be a bit scary, and may be the reason why she is suddenly so clingy and needy and why her moods swing from one extreme to the next.

Name emotions

Help your toddler to express her emotions by allowing her to use facial expressions to reflect her mood, and by ***naming*** the emotion: for example, " I can see from the scowl on your face that you are angry". Reassure her that it is OK to feel like that, and try and to distract her with an object or activity.

Sharing and taking turns

She will be very interested in other children, but will still play alongside, rather than **with** them. Don't expect her to have any idea about sharing or taking turns, unless you organise the activity. Praise her when she does share or take turns, and try to avoid always scolding her when she doesn't. Rather ***acknowledge*** that she is finding it difficult to share or take turns; this may make her more willing to do so.

She learns best by imitation now, so teach her to share and take turns by starting with sharing and taking turns with you, this will make it easier for her to follow by example.

Self-esteem

Any encouragement and involvement in any appropriate activities that she performs will boost her self-esteem enormously. Remember that self-esteem starts with **you**, the parents or caregivers. If you feel good about yourself, the feeling will rub off on your child. A healthy self-esteem provides your child with the best foundation for life.

Try your best to keep up with some child-centred floor-time every day if possible (see page 74).

PLAY FOR LIFE

"In the early formative years, play is almost synonymous with life. It is second only to being nourished, protected and loved. It is a basic ingredient of physical, intellectual, social and emotional growth". Ashley Montague (Anthropologist)

NUTRITION

Your toddler will need plenty of gentle encouragement to eat properly at this age. You can waste an enormous amount of energy forcing your stubborn, but well-nourished toddler to eat against her will! She may well prefer to eat small amounts five times a day, as opposed to fewer larger meals.

She will still need in the region of 500–600 ml of milk per day, divided into drinks and food. If she is not having iron-fortified milk, or has a poor appetite, it is a good idea to give her a multivitamin and iron supplement. Ask your health care provider to recommend one.

Her food should no longer be pureed, but rather chopped up into small pieces. See menu plan idea on page 83.

Sensible hydration

Water keeps the brain hydrated so that it can carry out the electrical and chemical reactions necessary to process all the sensory information it receives. If your child is thirsty, she will be more irritable as the central nervous system (including the brain) is the first place to get dehydrated. Offer her water throughout the day, especially if it is very hot. Don't go overboard though, as too much water can cause electrolyte imbalances and impair a healthy appetite for meals.

Table manners and socialisation

Keep her mealtimes calm and quiet and give her your full attention – she will be more likely to eat in this kind of environment than in a disorganised, noisy environment. It is a good idea to try to have at least one meal a day together as a family. Encourage table manners and socialisation at mealtimes.

Offer your toddler a small spoon or fork and encourage her to 'spear' her food onto her fork.

BEHAVIOUR

Your toddler is ready to start to learn some basic manners. This is the time to teach her to say 'the magic words' – *please* and *thank you.* Set a good example, and she will follow (remember that she learns from imitation). She will notice the pleased reaction of grown-ups when she says "please" and "thank you", and at least some of the time will use these words appropriately.

Don't expect her always to obey your instructions – just because she can understand them, does not mean that she will always carry them out !

Your toddler is developing a will of her own and the ***terrible twos*** are looming. She is still at the age where she is impulsive, passionate and has little self-control. She does not understand that screaming will not make the food come any faster (even though it worked when she was a baby), or that she will upset her playmate by snatching a toy away from him. Everything is 'mine', and nothing is 'yours'.

PLAN B

Try to show your pleasure when your toddler co-operates with you and complies with your requests, but be prepared to remove her from the situation if she won't.

Temper tantrums

This is the stage that temper tantrums start to occur. Tantrums are a normal by-product of the developing toddler. They always tend to occur at the worst possible time for you, usually when she does not have your full attention, or when she is feeling tired, hungry or in sensory overload (see Signals page 34). When your toddler is in the throes of a temper tantrum, explaining the consequences of her actions won't give you immediate results if she is passionately letting you know how she is feeling by hitting out at you in anger. The best way to handle a tantrum is to ignore it (see Dealing with temper tantrums page 61).

When it comes to discipline, explaining things in a reassuring voice, with lots of affection and physical contact, is a good habit to get into from the start, and will make it easier for her to stay calm when she needs to wait her turn or co-operate with you.

SENSE-ABLE SECRET

Offer your child a new idea when she is frustrated and unsure. This will help to lead her to a solution she has not thought of before.

SLEEP ISSUES

Your toddler will most likely still be happy in her cot for now. Only put her in a bed if she is climbing out of her cot, or is waking frequently at night due to lack of space. (See Chapter 11: Care and development 2–3 years, page 109 for tips on easy transition into a bed.) She may start to resist two sleeps during daytime, but will find it very difficult to make it through the late afternoon if she only sleeps once a day, as her awake time (before she reaches sensory overload) between sleeps is still only approximately 3½–4 hours. If this is the case, remember 'early to bed' (between 5:30 and 6 pm) and make a real effort to avoid too much stimulation at that time.

Separation anxiety

Separation anxiety may cause her to be more resistant at bedtime now and may cause some night wakings. Be sure to spend some extra time reassuring her and cuddling her at bedtime, and try to take some time out of your day to spend some special time with her. This is just a transient phase and should disappear in a short while. If bedtime battles and night wakings continue for a long period of time, then consider implementing some sleep training strategies (see page 40). At this age it is important to acknowledge and name her anxiety about going to sleep on her own and to offer plenty of reassurance. So you could say to her, "I know that you do not want to go to sleep because you are lonely, but it is OK, I will stay with you for a little while to make you feel better" (see Chapter 5: Sleep, page 37). Remember that if you are implementing sleep training, it is important that you always do come back to reassure her if you say you will. Keep her ***sensory environment*** calming in the period of time before bed and stick to a routine and bedtime rituals (see page 40).

OTHER ISSUES

One of the most significant issues affecting your toddler's life at this stage may be the arrival of a sibling.

Arrival of a sibling

It is often at this stage of your toddler's life that you may be expecting another baby. Expanding your family is exciting and a great cause of joy, but it won't be without its ups and downs! Here are some tips to prepare your toddler (and yourself) for the new baby.

KEEP IT LOW-KEY

If your toddler is still quite young (under the age of four) adopt a low-key attitude about the forthcoming arrival – she is still too little to understand the concept of pregnancy. A pre-school child is able to have more understanding. About three to four months before baby is due, tell her truthfully and directly about the coming birth (she will most likely be asking questions about the size of your tummy by now), but don't go overboard with too much detail unless she asks.

DON'T OVER-COMPENSATE

It is perfectly normal for you to be worried about managing to have enough love for another child, so don't fall into the trap of over compensating by allowing your toddler to always get her own way. Assure her that having another baby will not affect how much you love her.

DON'T DISRUPT YOUR TODDLER'S ROUTINE

If your toddler is in day care, or you can organise a babysitter, avoid taking her along with you when you go for your ante-natal check ups. You may have to wait for a long period of time before seeing the midwife or doctor, and it is unfair to expect your toddler to be happy and entertained in that environment. Use this time alone to start bonding with your unborn baby.

When you're in hospital to have the baby, keep your toddler's routine and structure at home unchanged. As long as she is happy and content in her home environment, and has adequate emotional support, she should take your absence in her stride.

INVOLVE YOUR TODDLER

Invite your toddler to help you shop for and set up the nursery; it will make her feel special and involved.

If you are planning a home birth, invite your midwife to come round with her equipment and spend some time explaining to your toddler what will happen when she arrives to take care of you.

PREPARE HER FOR YOUR ABSENCE

If you are going to hospital for the birth, prepare your toddler for your upcoming absence about two to three weeks before your due date. If she has never been separated from you, start to leave her with her dad or a sitter for a couple of hours a day. This way she will be used to your absence when the time comes. Dispel any fears and doubts that she may have by discussing the arrangements as clearly as possible. "Granny is coming to look after you while Mommy is in the hospital"). Keep her away from the hospital while you are there. You may be anxious about not seeing her for a few days, but it is more traumatic for her to have to say goodbye to you after visiting hours. She may not understand why you can't come home with her, or why she can't stay with you. Hospitals are also breeding grounds for all sorts of horrible germs, so don't expose your toddler to them unnecessarily.

COPING STRATEGIES WHEN YOU COME HOME

In the few weeks before the new baby is due, get organised – pre - cook meals and stock up your pantry so that you have more time to spend with the new baby and your toddler once the new baby is there. Follow the guidelines below for further coping tips once you are home:

- When you return home with the new baby, present your toddler with a gift from her new sibling. A doll with accessories is always a good idea even for boys!
- Your toddler will play up and demand your attention just when you can't give it, so expect her demands to intensify, especially if you have just sat down to feed the baby! To the best of your ability always attend to her needs first – this will make her feel secure.

- Have a pile of storybooks handy and place one of her little chairs alongside your feeding chair, so that she can sit with you and read a story when you feed the baby. This is a good habit to start, and she will start to look forward to this special time with you.
- When visitors arrive to see the new baby, let her show them to the nursery, and allow her to help open the baby's gift, this way she will feel included.
- Avoid saying, "Don't touch the baby" too much. She will cotton on that touching the baby gets your attention and will continue to do it. If possible, ignore it (unless she is feeding the baby a NikNak, or holding him upside down). Never leave her alone with the new baby.
- Use every bit of help offered.
- Take the phone off the hook when you are resting, or at least invest in a portable phone to keep alongside you.
- Limit visitors to a specific time of the day, so that you are not inundated all day. Visitors, while having your best interests at heart, can kill you with kindness. And if you are feeling frazzled, your toddler will sense this and become even more demanding.
- Stick to your toddler's routine scrupulously – it will make the whole family feel more secure.
- Expect a regression in your toddler's behaviour. She may demand a bottle or dummy again. Keep calm, give her what she asks for, and know that it will pass with time.
- Try to spend some special time alone with your toddler every day, even if it means quiet time in the garden for twenty minutes.
- Look after your relationship with your partner – remember that you are in this together, and your toddler will sense any tension.

POSITIVE ASSOCIATION

When you are still pregnant, put together a little box of age-appropriate wrapped goodies for her (for example a small box of smarties or a toy bottle), and keep this in the baby's room. When you are busy with the baby and cannot attend to your toddler (such as when you are changing a stinky nappy, or feeding), allow her to go to her 'special box' and select a present. The selection and the subsequent unwrapping and exploration will buy you the time you need to finish off your task. This way, she will only associate a positive experience with the fact that you are unable to attend to her immediately.

FLEXIBLE ROUTINE

- Your toddler should be eating from all the food groups spread over three to five small meals a day.
- She may have dropped her early morning milk drink, and may prefer to wait until breakfast time for her first drink.

- Limit her awake times between sleeps to 3½ - 4 hours and plan your care-giving outings and stimulation within this time.
- She may still need two sleeps a day, varying from 45 minutes to 2 hours. If she is only sleeping once a day, the sleep will vary from 60 minutes to 3 hours in duration.
- Bedtime should be between 6 and 7 pm depending on the last sleep in the afternoon.
- She should be sleeping for 13 – 14 hours in a 24 hour cycle.

ACTIVITIES AND TOYS TO ENHANCE DEVELOPMENT

Your toddler is still very dependent on her parents or caregivers for most stimulation, but will start to potter around happily on her own, as long as you are nearby, so that she can check up on you frequently. Encourage plenty of outdoor play such as running, jumping and climbing to stimulate her ***gross motor development***. This is the age where toddlers love to copy you in any activity, so swing your arms and legs, jump and hop and she will follow suit.

Any form of ***auditory stimulation*** is very important. Her auditory processing-skills are extremely important for school readiness and literacy, so don't leave it too late to start teaching her the difference between loud and soft sounds. Play with a drum – say the word 'loud' when you hit it hard, and 'soft' when you hit softly. Start to teach her different animal sounds from the environment. Remember to always time the activity for when the listening environment is ideal (no distractions), and not when she is tired or hungry. Listening to tapes and CDs, as well as making body sounds such as clapping hands or tapping feet will all stimulate her sense of hearing. Always maintain eye contact in whatever activity you are doing with her.

Balls remain a great hit – all shapes and sizes. Throw them, chase after them and roll them back and forth – this will help her to have an idea of how to control speed. Show her how to throw a small ball at a row of skittles – this will help her ***visual tracking skills.*** She will love to chase blown up balloons or bubbles (let her clap and pop bubbles) in the garden. Never leave a child alone with a balloon – it may pop and she could choke on the pieces.

Show her how to duck under tables and climb over the couch – this will help her learn about her ***body in space.*** Help her to walk slowly on the garden wall or a plank to enhance her balancing skills.

Kneading and pulling on play dough is great for ***fine motor-control*** and to stimulate her sense of ***touch.*** Anything that can stack, twist, turn, roll, fit together or come apart are great for stimulating ***fine muscle- control.*** Spread out large sheets of paper and let her finger paint, using both hands. Let her ***touch, taste*** and ***sniff*** new and different textures, food and smells. Bath time is a great opportunity to enhance all aspects of her development. A variety of sponges and loofahs can be used to encourage tolerance to touch. Squeezing the soap out of a sponge develops wrist and hand strength and stirring the bath water with both hands moving in opposite directions enhances co-ordination between the two sides of her body. Spraying her off with a vibrating shower head, or getting her to hold it herself will enhance the feedback to her muscles and joints, and develop the awareness of her body in space. Easy, simple ways of helping her ***sensory system*** develop whilst at the same time having fun!

See table on pages 28–30 for suggestions to calm or stimulate her **sensory system**.

Ideas for toys and equipment

- jungle gym
- trampoline
- swing
- hammock
- swingball
- wheelbarrow
- rocking horse
- balls of different sizes
- skittles (collect old tins and use them as skittles)
- balloons
- bubbles
- stacking cups and assorted canisters with lids
- shape sorters
- large beads
- knob puzzles
- simple construction toys
- an old wallet and a pile of old credit cards (wonderful for fine motor-skills)
- shopping trolley and accessories
- finger paint
- chunky crayons
- blackboard and chalk
- back of old calendar sheets
- music tapes or compact discs
- toy drum and tambourine
- books

These are some simple ideas to have fun with your toddler whilst at the same time enhancing her development. For more in-depth stimulation ideas try these books:

- *Clever talk* by Martie Pieterse (Metz Press. 1999)
- *School readiness through play* by Martie Pieterse (Metz Press. 2001)
- *Brain gym for all* by Melodie de Jager (Human & Rosseau. 2001)
- *Entertaining and educating babies and toddlers* by Roby Gee and Susan Meredith (Usborne. 1986)

TEETH

By the age of two years, your toddler should have in the region of 16 teeth, including the first molars. If you are experiencing restless nights due to teething, ask your clinic sister to recommend a teething remedy.

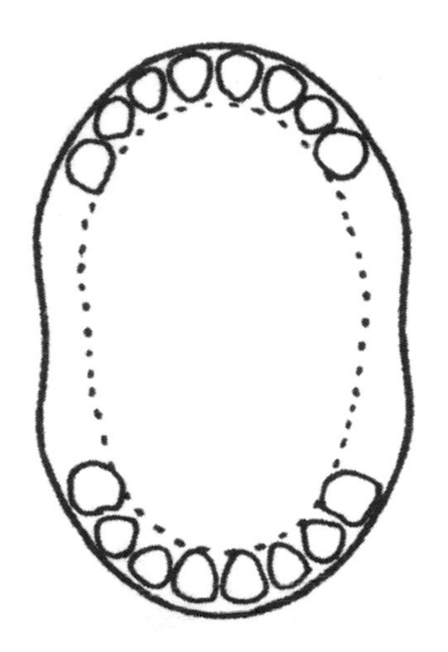

YOUR TODDLER'S FINE – HOW ARE YOU?

Just because your baby has grown up into a sturdy toddler, doesn't mean that you can't suffer from postnatal depression, especially if you've had another baby and great demands are being made on your time and attention. If you feel

- out of control, frustrated and very irritable;
- that you are not the kind of mother you want to be;
- scared, panicky, anxious and worried;
- sad or miserable most of the time;
- unable to laugh or to feel joy;
- unable to cope;
- afraid to be alone;
- unusually tearful;
- as though you are going crazy;

or if you have

- difficulty in sleeping;
- no sex drive;
- thoughts about harming yourself or your child;

you may be suffering from postnatal depression. Please seek help. The PNDSA provides education and support to health professionals and the public regarding emotional difficulties associated with child-bearing. Contact them on the PNDSA help lines: 082 882 0072 or 083 309 3960; or tel/fax: 021- 797 4498.

*If I had influence with the good fairy who is supposed to preside over
the christening of all children, I should ask that her gift to each child in the world
be a sense of wonder so indestructible that it would last throughout life.*

RACHEL CARSON

CHAPTER 11

Care and development 2-3 years

Toni marvels at how 'grown up' her two-year-old son has suddenly become. Rowan truly believes he owns the world and never seems to sit still for any length of time. It's almost as if he is thinking, "So much to see and do, and so little time to do it!" Toni is amazed at Rowan's independence at times and can't believe that Rowan will sometimes walk away from her without a second glance as he investigates this new and exciting world he has discovered. He is starting to become aware of the potty, and has even been successful a few times! Rowan has started having more temper tantrums lately, especially if he is tired or hungry, but Toni has made an effort to tune in to Rowan's signals and these sensory triggers, and tries her best to avoid situations likely to lead to such outbursts. Nevertheless, she finds coping with a busy and inquisitive two-year-old exhausting.

Two-year-olds are on a whirlwind voyage of mobility and discovery. Your little toddler has become a bigger toddler. He has taken two years to undergo the magical transformation from infancy to independence. His little body looks more 'grown up' with longer arms and legs and less baby fat. This tumultuous and exciting time of your toddler's life can lead to some interesting and challenging behaviours. He will fight for his independence by testing and pushing his (and your) limits wherever he can. "I can do it!" will become a common refrain, and he may insist on pouring his own juice, feeding himself and strapping himself into his car seat, even though it takes twice the amount of time.

This is the time when you will consider toilet or potty training your toddler. It is important to wait until he is showing signs of being ready **before** you begin. Be relaxed about toilet training, and more importantly, keep your sense of humour (see Chapter 6: Toilet or potty training, page 51).

LANGUAGE DEVELOPMENT

From now on, your toddler accumulates vocabulary at a rapid rate. By now he should be saying up to 200–300 words, either in their single form, or by constructing the odd sentence with two to three words. He will begin to use words such as "mine" and "I" and "you" and "yours".

His receptive speech (what he understands) will still be far superior to his expressive speech (what he can say), so don't stop talking to him all the time. Research has shown that children of this age with talkative mothers have a larger vocabulary than children growing up hearing less of the spoken word.

Your toddler should be able to recognise and identify familiar objects and understand simple questions and commands, which he will be able to carry out. For example you would say, "Where are granny's glasses? There they are, thank you, will you please pass them to granny? ". When he speaks, don't worry if his sentences are a bit muddled. As he progresses, he will make more sense, as he learns to use his words in the correct order. By the time Rowan is two and a half, he can say ***who*** he is and name his body parts – for example, "Rowan's tummy". He may even be able to start using simple adjectives such as 'big' or 'small'.

Your toddler's listening skills will be improving, and he will love listening to stories. (Keep them short and sweet!) Don't worry if he can't remember the story later. Get used to having plenty of patience on tap, as this is the age when he will begin to ask, "What …?" and "Where …" and "Why …?" frequently! Follow his cue and ask him questions to encourage him to use his rapidly increasing language skills.

This is really the age that your child's language development takes off. Language is the crucial axis of all intellectual development and further learning. Everything he has learnt, and will still learn, revolves around language. Never underestimate the important role you play in this vital part of his development.

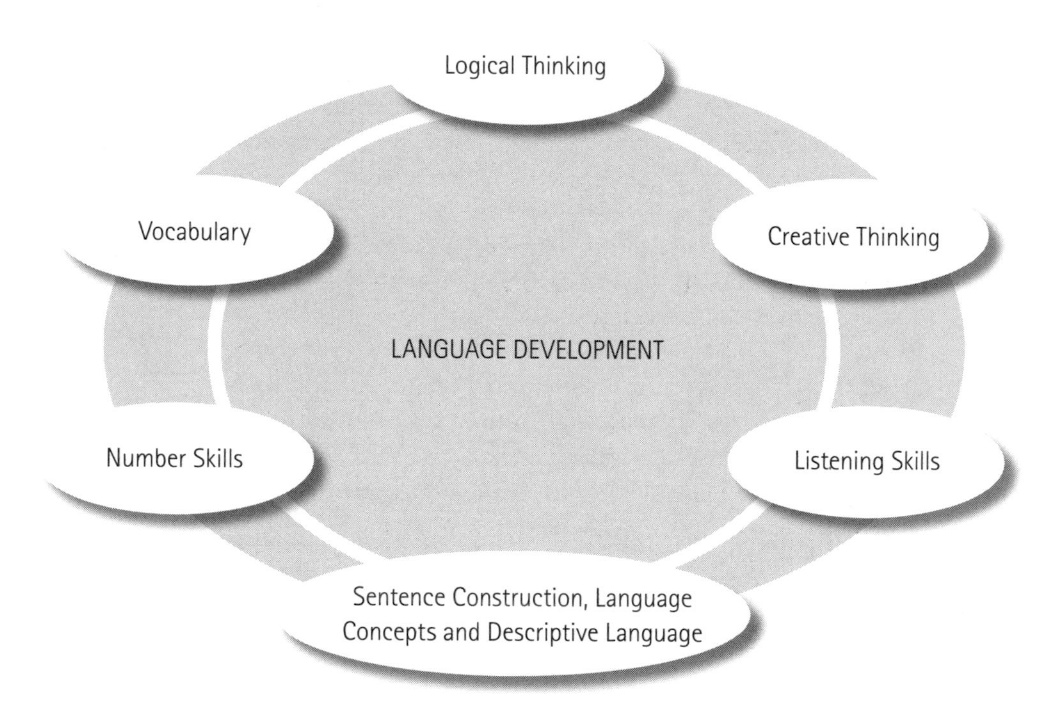

(Adapted from *School readiness through play* by Martie Pieterse, Metz Press).

MOTOR DEVELOPMENT

While trying out new experiences from his world by using his sensory system, Rowan is becoming aware of the *limitations* of his new-found powers. He will climb up the jungle gym and not know how to get down, and will become tangled in his jersey when he insists on dressing himself.

Your toddler should be able to run and walk on his whole foot by now (no more tip-toeing) and shouldn't fall over when throwing a small ball. His *sense of balance* has progressed to the extent that he can stand on one leg for a few seconds by the time he is three. He will be able to walk up stairs, but may still need some help coming down. When playing with objects on the floor, he will squat for long periods of time and will be able to stand up again without support. He will be able to ride a toy motorbike without falling off, and will also be able to change direction whilst riding on it by pushing with his feet.

His *fine-motor skills* are improving, and he will be able to open drawers and turn handles with dexterity, scribble with a crayon, begin to cut with scissors as well as handle his food and drink without spilling. He may enjoy doing simple puzzles, and can build a tower of six or more blocks. He will start to use one side of his body more frequently than the other for tasks that require some skill, such as brushing his hair and reaching for objects. By the time he turns three, your toddler should have a hand (and foot) preference for skilled fine-motor tasks such as drawing.

EMOTIONAL DEVELOPMENT

Your toddler now has the ability to express emotions with words. So, instead of the nuclear fallout, screaming fits and floor thrashing episodes, he may tell you, "Go away" or "Don't want it".

Criticism and approval

He will still be hurt by criticism, but will start to become less negative and argumentative. He will still always seek your approval in all that he does, but be warned, his behaviour will move from wanting to please you to being downright difficult by wanting to control you and whoever else is around. Talk about his emotions when you chat to him. Try to avoid quizzing him with only memory questions ("What did you do at play school today?"), and try to be purposeful in your inclusion of emotional questions ("What was *fun* at playschool today?"). Or if you notice he looks upset when you fetch him, instead of saying, "What happened?", you could try saying, "Did anybody make you sad today?"

Child's play

By playing games with him when it comes to chores (such as packing away toys) he will come to understand that part of gaining independence and growing up will mean that he has to agree with and work with you on certain issues. Whilst being both frustrated and frightened by this new learning curve, he is, however, taking the first tentative steps towards developing his own identity. Fantasy and pretend play really comes into its own at this stage, and he may use it to escape from difficult realities he is facing in real life. When you spend time with him during your special floor-time play, and you are always the 'bad guy', ask him a lot of "Why?" questions and try to encourage an emotional response. If there are any underlying emotions such as loss, competition or aggression, this type of play will help him to work through any unresolved issues he may have.

Wandering

Your toddler now has the physical and mental capacity to wander off on his own, so it will seem as though you are forever trotting off after him to protect him from harm as he explores his world. He is, however, still worried about abandonment, and may display some signs of separation anxiety at times. This is a completely normal phase of development at this stage, so don't worry if he does have times when he is clingy and needy and won't let you out of his sight.

NUTRITION

Two-year-olds are notorious for flexing their emotional muscles, and they quickly realize that eating and food (or refusing it) is an area where they have plenty of control. As you know by now, if your toddler senses your anxiety at mealtimes, food may soon become a psychological battleground. Try to relax and rather motivate your child to eat by not forcing him, and letting him eat what he wants to, excluding junk food of course (see Chapter 9, page 82).

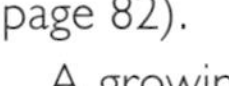

A growing-up milk or vitamin supplement with iron will ensure that your toddler gets all the nutrients that he needs but avoid replacing meals with milk. If you take note of what your toddler eats over a period of time (say a week), you will be pleasantly surprised to find that it is actually quite a balanced diet.

His previously rapid growth has slowed down, but his protein and energy needs are still very important, so try to include in the region of four tablespoons of protein foods (meat, dairy, beans, fish, poultry, eggs) in his meals in the course of the day. Calcium-rich foods are also important, and he will need four small servings (1 tablespoon equals 1 serving) of cheese, yoghurt or milk in a day.

Try to include another four servings of fruit or vegetables somewhere during the day. These could be in the form of some grated or chopped fruit or raw vegetables given as a snack (bite-sized pieces to make it more appetizing), or mix fruit and yoghurt or ice cream together to make a smoothie. Disguise vegetables into sauces and minced meat if your toddler refuses to eat them.

AL FRESCO

For a change of scenery, take a picnic into the garden or make a tent under the dining room table and invite a playmate to share in the fun. Toddlers emulate their peers and eat quickly when they see others doing so, especially if the occasion is a novelty.

BEHAVIOUR

Your toddler's newly developed sense of independence can be trying for you, so be prepared to deal with some interesting behaviour patterns. Be reassured, however, that he is not being difficult on purpose, but is rather finding a way of developing his own sense of self.

Control

Your toddler will happily play alongside another child (parallel play), but is still not ready for any co-operative play. He is still a very self-centred little person who only sees things from his point of view. He will still protest at having to share anything, and will take control of activities and toys at the drop of a hat. This will change though, as he gets closer to his third birthday, when he will start to understand the concept of 'give and take'.

This realisation on his part, will make playtime a lot less stressful for you, as you won't have to play referee quite as often. He will love to play rough and tumble, even if it does sometimes end in tears.

It is important to allow him this time, as apart from the benefit to his sensory and motor development, he will learn about what is fun (arm wrestling), and what is not (getting hurt).

Nasty habits

Two year olds are notorious for developing some **nasty habits** such as hitting, kicking and biting. As you already know, some of these behaviours are sensory based, as they usually occur when your toddler is feeling tired and overwhelmed by his environment. (See Signals Chapter 4, pages 32–34 and Chapter 9 Care and development 15–18months pages 84–87.) Remember to try to always *acknowledge* his feelings of anger, but he does need to be told that what he did is *not* acceptable behaviour, and that it hurt the victim and the victim's feelings.

Fears and anxieties

Your toddler may develop some **fears and anxieties.** It is quite normal for him to become fearful of things like dogs or the vacuum cleaner. If he is showing some signs of anxiety, don't worry; it's a natural occurrence to help protect him from danger and will help him to cope with all the new experiences that are happening to him as he explores his world.

However, there are a few simple strategies that you can implement to help ease his fears.

ACKNOWLEDGE HIS FEARS

To you his fears and anxieties may seem silly, but to him they are very real and serious. Don't hope that if you ignore his fears that they will go away. For example, you could say to your child, " I know that you are frightened of the dog. Hold my hand and I will walk with you."

USE A 'COMFORT FRIEND'

If your toddler is anxious about going to playschool, allow him to take a favourite comfort object along. Tell him that it is there to make him feel better. As he gets older he will be able to find other ways to self-soothe and self-calm when he feels anxious and scared.

EXPLAIN, SHOW AND INVESTIGATE

If you provide a simple and rational explanation about a certain event, the chances are that he will overcome his fear pretty soon. So if he is petrified of being sucked up in the vacuum cleaner, explain to him that only very small objects can get sucked up, but not big objects like people. Demonstrate this to him by showing him the difference.

LEAD BY EXAMPLE

Even though language development is progressing rapidly, your toddler is still taking most of his behavioural cues from what he sees, not from spoken commands.

NEVER LIE

If a past experience is fuelling his fear (such as an immunisation), don't tell him that it won't hurt this time. Rather tell him that it will be a little bit sore, but that it is important that he has it done. Tempt him with the offer of something special afterwards. Don't let him pick up any anxiety and fear from your side – remain firm and in control.

USE PLAY

Role play whatever it is that he is fearful of. So if he is scared of strangers, encourage him to act out meeting strangers with his own toys.

BE BRAVE

Downplay your own fears. If your child sees you shrieking and having a fit when you see a spider, he will also be fearful of spiders. So try to work through your own fears, or at least pretend!

GET HELP

If your toddler's fears start to interfere with his normal day to day activities, and if they are intensifying with time, speak to your clinic sister or paediatrician, as he may have a genuine phobia about certain issues. If that is the case, psychological help is recommended.

SLEEP ISSUES

Even though your 'little' toddler is growing up into a 'big' toddler, he still needs plenty of sleep. At this stage he will most likely only sleep once a day, usually over lunch time.

SENSE-ABLE SECRET

Sticking to a flexible routine (page 112), watching his sensory cues (page 33) and disciplining when appropriate (page 59) will all contribute to a pleasant and relaxed journey for you all through the terrible twos.

New sleep zone

This is also the time when he outgrows his cot and makes the transition into a big bed. Invest in a side bar, and position his bed against a wall or chest of drawers. Let him help you select new linen for his bed (if necessary) and involve him in preparing his new room. Expect there to be some high jinks at bedtime the first few nights as he will be very excited about the novelty of the occasion. He may experience some restless nights whilst he gets used to sleeping in a larger space, so don't be alarmed if he wakes during the night on occasion. Remain firm, loving and consistent about bedtime rules and night wakings (see Chapter 5: Sleep, pages 40–42), and the transition will be pain free.

Lunch-time nap

Most toddlers this age can manage a short morning of activity, but towards lunchtime become overtired and ***over-stimulated***. He can manage about four to five hours of awake time before he needs a nap, so if your toddler is at play school, try to fetch him before 12 noon, so that you have time to get home before the wheels fall off.

Expect him to protest at having to go to sleep in the middle of the day, especially if he has just started at playschool – the novelty of it all may be too much. So ensure that there is always quiet time before his nap to allow him some ***time to unwind***. Close the curtains and keep his environment as ***calm*** as possible. Some children need only an hour to recharge, whilst others will sleep for up to three hours.

As long as he is waking up refreshed and in a good mood, is able to sustain a pleasant disposition for the afternoon activities, and there is a no fuss bedtime, then you can be assured that he is having a long enough day nap. If he is waking up grumpy, and the afternoon and evening is fraught with tension, you can be assured that his day nap is not long enough.

Try limiting the awake time between naps even more (even if it means that playschool falls by the wayside for a while), and keep your afternoons quiet and restful with an early bedtime routine. As he catches up on more sleep, you will be able to resume your previous routine. If delayed bedtimes and frequent night wakings are beginning to impact on your relationships and your health , consider implementing some sleep strategies as discussed in the Chapter 12: Care and development 3–4 years (see page 119).

OTHER ISSUES

Now that your toddler moves with ease and confidence he will want to explore as much as possible of the world around him. Encourage this and try to ensure that he retains his natural curiosity and spirit of adventure. Give him every opportunity to play and learn.

Playschool

Attending a playschool from a young age is by no means essential, but by the age of three, your toddler may begin to feel the need to interact with other children of a similar age. For countless working parents with children being cared for in crèche or day-care, the dilemma of when to send their toddler to playschool is not an issue – they are already happily ensconced in a system that is working for them. But for those toddlers who are at home, either with a nanny, or a stay-at-home mom, there may come a time when he needs to learn to socialise and play with other children. Sending your child to playschool may be the first significant separation between you and him, so it is important to take into account your child's temperament and your home environment. Some two-year-olds are quite happy and stimulated in the home environment – these children usually have siblings at home with them or live with an extended family, or attend parent-tot workshops and outings frequently. Other two-year-olds lack stimulation in the home environment and are bored, lonely and frustrated. This may manifest in behaviour that is perceived as naughtiness.

It is important to remember that most two-year-olds don't really play ***with*** other children, but rather play ***alongside*** them. They don't really have an idea of sharing, turn taking and organised play activities. For this reason it is important that the playschool you choose is really that – a safe ***play environment*** with the emphasis on having fun. The bonus for your child (provided he is ready) is that playschool is the perfect platform for emotional and social development at the same time as simply having fun.

The following list can serve as a guideline as to when your toddler may be **ready** for playschool:

- He can play happily alongside another child.
- He starts to show some sense of responsibility for his belongings.
- He can separate from you without undue stress and remains secure when parent or caregiver is not present.

- He can generally communicate his needs.
- He has enough confidence to ask for help.
- He is used to relating to other adults.
- He is either potty trained, or has a definite awareness of toilet training.
- He is able to initiate play and will play on his own.

IT MUST BE FUN

Playgroup is not meant to be an anxious experience for your child, so if your child is struggling to settle in and is still miserable after a few weeks, consider taking him out of the school and waiting a few more months before trying again.

CHOOSING A PLAYSCHOOL OR GROUP

- Go by word of mouth – this is by far the best referral system.
- Look for a playgroup that is small – no more than 10 children in a group.
- Ensure that the children are all roughly the same age.
- Check that the playgroup area is safe and secure and toddler-friendly.
- Ensure that the nappy changing area is kept scrupulously clean, and that there are adequate potties or small toilets and hand-washing facilities for toilet training.
- Pop in unexpectedly on a few occasions – if the children always look happy and the teacher is too, it's a sure bet!

Worms

Worm infestation is common, but is often ignored by parents or caregivers as it is such an unpleasant thought. Worm eggs are so small that they cannot be seen with the naked eye. You can breathe them in, swallow them, or pick them up on your skin without even knowing it. The symptoms are not always obvious but as the worm load increases, your child may display some of these signs and symptoms:

- poor appetite and weight loss;
- irritability and sleeplessness;
- itching and redness around the anus;
- vomiting, constipation or mild diarrhoea, abdominal pain;
- blood or worms in the stool;
- slight fever;
- anaemia and tiredness;
- itching of the skin between the toes.

Children with chronic worm infestation are more prone to infection and often appear to be 'pale and peaky'. Toddlers are very susceptible to parasite (worm) infestation simply due to the nature of their busy lives, so it is important to instil good personal hygiene habits from a young age (such as washing your hands after touching an animal and before meals). It is recommended that all toddlers (from the age of 2 years) as well as the whole household (including pets) be regularly de-wormed. Ask your healthcare provider to suggest a de-worming preparation. Prevention is better than cure, so remember to repeat the dosage as recommended.

FLEXIBLE ROUTINE

- Your toddler should be eating from all the food groups (not necessarily in one day if they are picky eaters) spread over three to five small meals a day.
- His milk will consist of one to two cups of growing-up milk or full cream cow's milk per day, drunk out of a cup or a bedtime bottle.
- He will still need one sleep a day, varying in duration from one to three hours, usually in the late morning.
- Limit his awake time between sleeps to 4–5 hours and plan your care-giving, playschool, outings and stimulation within this time.
- He can occasionally miss a day-time sleep owing to an important event.
- Bedtime should be between 6 and 7 pm depending on what time he awakens from his day sleep.
- He should be sleeping through the night for a period of 10 – 12 hours.
- He should be sleeping for 13–14 hours in a 24 hour cycle.

ACTIVITIES AND TOYS TO ENHANCE DEVELOPMENT

Encourage your toddler to spend as much time outdoors as possible. Running, jumping, climbing and swinging are all excellent for ***gross-motor development,*** as well as for enhancing his sense of movement and balance. Offer him a variety of different sized objects to manipulate, thread and stack. Show him how to use a pair of little pre-school scissors to learn to cut – this will help with ***fine-motor development.*** (Watch out for him cutting your curtains and linen to shreds – rather supervise him when he uses scissors!).

He will love to pour mix, sieve and mould, and is starting to draw shapes (especially circles). Pillow fights in a safe zone using a few small cushions or soft toys are a great way to develop ***hand-eye co-ordination.***

To enhance his ***visual perception and discrimination,*** show him the differences between objects such as different fruits and vegetables and encourage him to sort them into colours or types. Let him practise these skills by showing him how to pack his toys away in the toy box – cars in one container, blocks in another and so on!

Toddlers of this age love helping around the house. Let him help sort the ironing into categories, for example matching socks, or ask him to put all the T-shirts together so you can fold them.

As he becomes more aware of his ***own position in space,*** and how he is moving, he will be able to push and pull objects in front of, and behind him, so he will be able to push a toy wheelbarrow, or drag a plastic chair behind him. Encourage him to play with a sit-and-ride or a tricycle, and show him how to change direction whilst riding. Another activity to help develop his sense of where things are in space is to teach your toddler that the top of the stove is always the top, and that the bottom and sides are positions that will always be there in relation to the top. Show him that by stacking blocks one on top of the other he can build a tower, but if he lays them side by side, he can build a train.

To have fun with your toddler whilst enhancing his *language and listening skills*, imitate sounds as they happen and point out *specific* sounds as they happen (for example, a dog barking). Hand-clapping games are great fun. Say a few names with his name in between and let him clap his hands when he hears his name. At first you will have to hold his hands and clap them each time you say his name, but you will be amazed at how quickly he will catch on. Obviously, talking, talking, talking is a cheap and easy way to develop language and listening skills, as well as letting him join you singing simple songs and rhymes. When you read stories show him that hands, feet and bottoms remain still and that we listen with our ears. Cup your hands around your ears to demonstrate what listening is. Also encourage him to look at books on his own.

Expose him to different textures, food and smells to enhance his sense of *taste, smell* and *touch*. See table on pages 28–30 for suggestions to calm or stimulate his sensory system.

These are some simple ideas to have fun with your toddlers whilst at the same time enhancing his development. For more in-depth stimulation ideas try these books:

- *Clever talk* by Martie Pieterse (Metz Press. 1999)
- *School readiness through play* by Martie Pieterse (Metz Press. 2001)
- *Brain gym for all* by Melodie de Jager (Human & Rosseau. 2001)
- *Entertaining and educating babies and toddlers* by Roby Gee and Susan Meredith (Usborne. 1986)

Ideas for age-appropriate toys and equipment

- climbing apparatus
- swing and slide
- jungle gym
- black plastic motor-bike or sit-and-ride toy
- tricycle
- plastic cricket or golf set
- building blocks
- cars, trains, trucks, planes, boats
- playdough and accessories (see playdough recipe page 137)
- buckets and spades
- rakes
- watering can
- sieves, moulds, waterwheels

- finger paint
- crayons
- tool set and workbench
- toy vacuum cleaner, ironing board, brush and dustpan
- toy gardening tools
- musical instruments (drum, keyboard, bells)
- music tapes or compact discs
- videos such as *Barney*

TEETH

Your toddlers last (second) molars should be out by now. The bottom two usually cut first, followed by the two at the top. These molars are his largest teeth, and will enable him to really chew his food well. By the time your toddler is three years old, he should have 20 teeth. 10 at the top and 10 at the bottom.

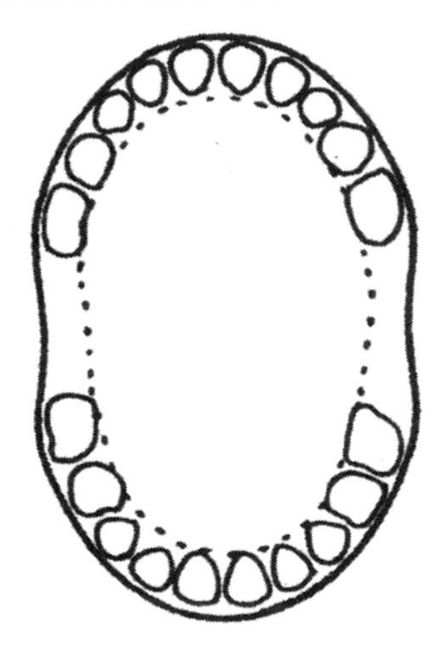

TEACH HIM TO SWIM

This is the time to consider teaching your child to swim. This is a lovely way to have some fun time together, and for your child to get used to being in water. The added advantage is that, with time, your child will become swim safe. Until such time, though, ensure that all safety procedures are in place whenever there is a swimming pool or open pond in your environment, such as safety nets, fencing, and vigilance. For contact details of specialised and reputable swimming teachers in your area contact the Professional Baby Swimming Teachers Association (PBSTA) 011 454 1413; 012 661 7890, or the Professional Swimming Teachers and Coaches Association (PSTCA) 011 786 2744.

All that I am or hope to be I owe to my angel mother.
Abraham Lincoln

CHAPTER 12

Care and development 3-4 years

Michelle is excited to be going to play at teacher Gay's, and eagerly arrives for her first day at nursery school. Despite being a bit shy at first, she happily wanders off to investigate the interesting-looking toys, and seems confident and secure in her new surroundings. Michelle's mom, Gill, is not so sure. Michelle has been at home with her for the past three years, and they have a close bond. But Gill realizes that it is time for Michelle to broaden her horizons, develop some new and necessary social skills and learn some independence.

Your little big toddler is now developing into a 'grown up' toddler, and is learning that she is independent from you. It has taken her three years to learn to roll, sit, crawl, walk, run, jump and climb; not to mention all the other skills that she has mastered, like talking and listening. Guess what? This may be the time that you can leave home without packing up the whole house, as the chances are that your toddler is now toilet trained during the day, and is most likely becoming dry at night too. Michelle is learning how to wash and dress herself, and can brush her own teeth and Gill is relieved that she is using a fork and spoon to feed herself now, so mealtimes are no longer the messy affair they used to be.

LANGUAGE DEVELOPMENT

Your little lady will have an expressive vocabulary of up to 500 words and be able to chat in sentences of six or more words. She carries on a simple conversation, asks questions (those dreaded why's and where's and when's again!) and chats about what she has seen or done – even with strangers ("Hey Lady, you know what ...?".) Michelle speaks well enough for strangers to understand her and is starting to use '-s' on verbs to show the present tense such as when she says, "Mommy *runs* after me". She also begins to use plurals and will often talk to herself or an imaginary friend.

It is important, now, to foster and strengthen her listening skills. As you will see from the diagram on the next page, good listening skills are the precursor to satisfactory life skills.

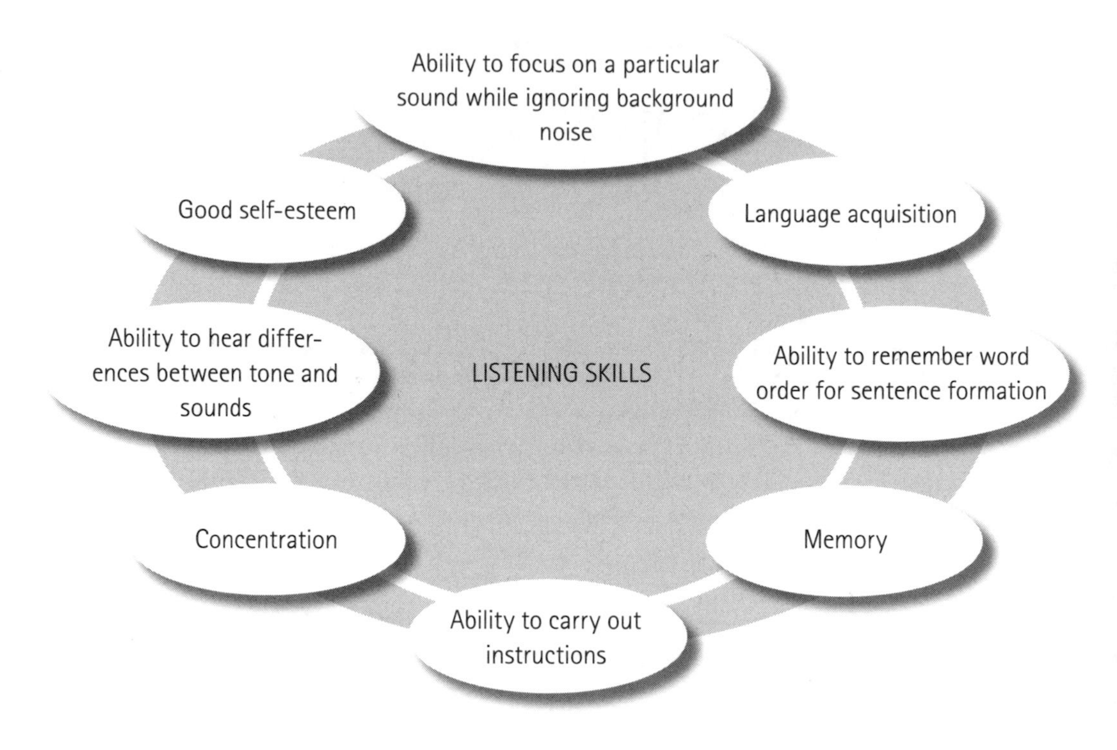

Importance of listening skills

Checklist for hearing

- By now your toddler will be able to use a two to three word sentence at least and should confidently ask for things and talk about her activities.
- She should be able to follow simple directions.
- She should be able to follow more complex instructions.
- She should begin to understand the difference between 'not now' and 'no more'.
- If your toddler has suffered from repeated ear infections and has difficulty with hearing and balance – seek professional advice.

HEARING TEST

If you are worried about your child's hearing, it is a good idea to take her for a hearing test with a qualified audiologist, preferably with paediatric experience. For details of an audiologist in your area, contact The South African Speech Language and Hearing Association (012) 653-2114 or www.saslha.co.za.

MOTOR DEVELOPMENT

This is a really fun time! Your toddler (now quite grown up) will be able to climb a jungle gym with agility; ride a tricycle quite fast (and speed around corners too); walk on tiptoe and stand on one foot. She can manage to go up and down stairs without help, and will love to jump from the bottom step with a flourish! She can wash her own hands when necessary, and will be able to undress herself if she wants. Dressing may still take a while, particularly if there are fiddly collars and fastenings, or if you are in a hurry!

She will be able to build a tower of nine to twelve blocks, and as she gets closer to four years of age will manage intricate construction toys. She will be able to draw a figure that resembles a person, with a head and maybe some features such as sticking out hands, or large eyes. By the age of four she will draw a body with arms and legs in the right places. By now she should be familiar with the names of her various body parts. She is starting to have an awareness of matching shapes and colours, and understands simple concepts of size and numbers.

As she encounters new information, she will move to embody it in all her muscles and senses. In other words, when she discovers something new (particularly if it is a large object such as a tree trunk) she will actually move her body to conform with the physical configuration of the new object to better understand it. So it stands to reason that this is a very physical and 'touchy' age. She seems to be unable to 'see' something unless she has 'touched' it. This is part of normal development, and should be encouraged whenever possible. It underlines the importance of enabling your toddler to experience life through as many senses as possible to enhance learning on all levels.

EMOTIONAL DEVELOPMENT

Your toddler will be less dependent on you by now – this is a good and positive sign that she is feeling more secure in her world. She will start to develop friendships independent of you. Separation anxiety should be a thing of the past by now, but don't be surprised if your toddler has temporary episodes of separation anxiety from time to time, especially if she has a timid, shy or anxious temperament.

Allow her some independence by letting her dress herself (no matter how long it takes) and don't squash burgeoning independence by intervening and saying, "Let me do it". This will only foster dependence on you, and diminish her confidence. Some children, when faced with a frustrating task, need time to problem solve on their own, without you rushing in to show or tell them *how to* do it. Your toddler may need some time to stop, suck her fingers and look away while she makes a plan to tackle the task more successfully.

Your toddler is now able to play and interact *with* playmates, and is able to understand the concept of give and take, turn taking and sharing. As she experiences her world, she is taking in a collage of images from her environment *via her sensory system*. Her subsequent responding actions all run though an emotional filter in her brain (as it has since birth). This constantly developing part of her brain is what enables your toddler to begin to form relationships and social bonds. Her emotions are what help her to interpret her experiences to enable her to organize her view of the world and her place in it.

It is at this age that your toddler will be able to *show concern and awareness* for another child's or adult's needs, and she will enjoy helping you with simple chores. She is beginning to see things in context for the first time.

Her *sense of identity* is stronger now, and this new-found awareness will help her to understand ownership ("This is mine, and that is yours"), her relationships and her place in society("This is *my* daddy"). She will also start to move from only experiencing possessiveness in terms of relationships and objects to having an *idea* of caring for the possession or person. For example, she will show concern that her playmate is sad, or has lost a toy. As your toddler's brain matures, nerve networks connect to her emotions and memory is established (see Chapter 2: Perceptual development, page 23–24).

IMAGINE THAT!

Imagination is more important than knowledge; while knowledge points to all there is, imagination points to all there will be.

Albert Einstein

NUTRITION

Remember that you are responsible for keeping healthy, nutritious food in the house and for offering it to your toddler. Let her help you shop for, choose, and prepare her food and she will show much more of an interest in eating it at mealtimes. Sit at the table with her at mealtimes, and try to have at least one family meal a day – this is how she will learn table manners. She should be able to feed herself by now and use a spoon and a fork with ease.

Avoid packing convenience and junk food into her playschool lunch box. Rather pack healthy sandwiches, rice cakes, fruit, raisins or date balls. Avoid sweetened or fizzy drinks, and encourage her to drink plenty of water. Bear in mind that a healthy diet for your toddler at this age is pretty much similar to a healthy adult diet – one that has plenty of fruit and vegetables (even if they are disguised!), complex carbohydrates (wholewheat bread, cereal, brown rice), enough protein and fat and sufficient calcium (milk, cheese and yoghurt – avoid fat free or low fat varieties until she is at least five years of age) and limited sugar, salt and refined, processed food. If you have a fussy eater, keep reminding yourself, as long as your toddler is healthy and thriving, that she will not voluntarily starve herself!

BEHAVIOUR

At times your toddler will be so flooded with emotion it will seem that she has been invaded by an alien force! Big feelings happen to little people, and she will be happy and content one moment, but sobbing the next, lying on the floor with her legs and arms pumping with anger. Forget the ***terrible twos***, it is the ***tricky threes*** that really will test your patience to the limit! As she gets closer to her fourth birthday, she will get very bossy, and you will soon see why the old adage 'all Chiefs and no Indians' applies to any four-year-old group at nursery school!

Teaching delayed gratification:

Your toddler will have a hard time learning to wait for something that she wants. We often give in and give our children what they want, ***when*** they want it as a way to avoid conflict and discipline issues. This deprives them of the opportunity to learn about delayed gratification, which is a very important part of learning to control emotions. When your toddler asks for a snack, say, "Of course you can have one. I will give it to you in a minute". Set a timer, and after a minute is up, give her the snack. Lengthen the period of time on each occasion. When she realizes that her needs ***will*** be met, she will develop a sense of time and learn delayed gratification. This is a lesson that will serve her well for the rest of her life.

SLEEP ISSUES

Your older toddler will definitely be sleeping in a bed now, and night wakings should be a long and distant bad memory! However, as your princess can still be very emotionally vulnerable from time to time, there may be nights where things go a bit awry. Bedtime battles or wakeful nights will usually occur if she is frightened (when there is a thunderstorm, for example), ill, or there is a change in her environment such as a new house. Letting her sleep alongside your bed on a little mattress or some continental pillows for a few nights usually does the trick, and with plenty of love and reassurance, she should soon re-establish her good sleeping habits. However, if she, in fact, had no good sleeping habits from the word go, or a transient sleeping disruption becomes a new habit, then it may be time to take the matter in hand - especially if it is beginning to impact on your relationships and your health.

Sleep training for bedtime battles

If you are having to lie or sit with your toddler until she falls asleep, try these strategies: Always

- **acknowledge** how she feels;
- then **mirror** the feeling;
- then give her a **reason** for your decision.

So, if she needs you to lie with her to go to sleep, say to her that you ***know*** that she wants you to, and that you would ***also*** like to lie with her, but you can't ***because*** you have a sore head, or things to do – offer her an alternative by saying that you will sit with her for a while, or hold her hand. Gradually wean yourself away from her by moving to the foot of the bed, and then a chair in the room, then hovering in the room, then popping in and out.

If she pushes beyond the boundary that you have set, by arguing and crying, move to the next stage of sleep training, which is to threaten to leave the room unless she stops arguing with you. If she complies, stay with her a bit longer and give her an extra hug, then try to leave again after a minute or two.

Be patient, it will work! If she persists in her arguing and crying, ***walk your talk*** and go, even if she protests! Go back and reassure her in a short while (after a minute or two), then repeat the process.

Gradually extend the amount of time spent out of her room (by one to two minutes) so that she is on her own for longer and longer periods of time. With time (and this may be from one session to the next, or it may take a few days), she will realize that you have not abandoned her, and that you are still around (albeit on your terms). She will be reassured by this realization, and will soon master the skill of getting to sleep by herself. It is very important to be consistent in your approach and not to confuse her with mixed messages.

GET RID OF THE MONSTERS

Fantasy and reality often merge at night time, especially at this age. If your toddler has fears such as monsters, do take her fears seriously, and do whatever it takes to chase them away.

OTHER ISSUES

When your little big toddler reaches the age of four it may be time to look at a more structured environment to enhance her intellectual development.

Going to nursery school

The modern trend is to enrol your toddler at a nursery school from three or four years of age. She may have attended a playschool from an earlier age, or may have been happy and content at home with you until now. While most playschools focus mostly on socialising and playing (for younger toddlers), nursery schools differ in that learning takes place in a more formal and structured way. Many nursery schools have separate classes or sections for different age groups, so try to find one that will allow for your child's progress without having to move her.

Trust your instinct when looking for a school, and decide whether the school will suit you and your toddler's needs with regard to accessibility, safety and hygiene and quality of teaching and care. Your toddler will still spend the better part of her time at nursery school playing, but now her play has themes and structure that are the perfect platform for emotional and social development. Your child will 'graduate to' pre-school when he turns five or six years. Most nursery schools have a pre-school class, so there may be no need to move your child before starting 'big school'.

IS YOUR CHILD READY?

It is usually around the age of three to four years, that your child seems ready to broaden her social horizons and interact with other children. However, there are a few criteria that you need to look at to determine whether your child is socially, emotionally, physically and cognitively ready to participate in a structured daily educational programme with a group of other children. A child who is ready for nursery school, meets the following cirteria:

Is fairly independent, and able to spend time away from you

Nursery school requires children to have certain basic skills; most will want your child to be potty-trained, for instance. Your child should also be able to take care of some other basic needs, like washing her hands after painting, eating her lunch without assistance, and sleeping alone. She should have mastered basic dressing and undressing, though she may need help with more fiddly things such as buttons and zips.

If your child has been cared for by a babysitter or a relative, she'll be better prepared to separate from you when she's at nursery school. Children who are used to being apart from their parents find the transition to nursery school relatively easy. If your child hasn't had many opportunities to be away from you, it may be an idea to start to have some time apart from you – a day with your sister and her kids, or an afternoon with granny.

Don't worry too much though, as most children leave Mom or Dad for the first time to go to nursery school and they do just fine. The trick is to help your child adjust in short doses. Many nursery schools will allow you to drop off your child for an hour or two during her first few days there. As she gets more used to her environment, you can gradually work up to a full day. Nursery school may even be more important for kids who've been at home with their parents, to help get them ready for the move to 'big school'.

Can work on projects on her own

Nursery school usually involves lots of arts and crafts projects that require concentration and the ability to focus on an individual task. If your child likes to draw at home or gets engrossed in puzzles and other activities on her own, she's a good candidate for preschool. But even if she's the kind of child who asks for help with everything, you can start getting her ready by setting up playtimes where she can entertain herself for a half hour or so. While you wash the dishes, encourage her to make creatures out of clay, for example. Gradually build up to longer stretches of solo play. Your goal here is to keep yourself moderately preoccupied with an activity so that she'll get on with her own without too much hand-holding from you.

Is ready to participate in group activities

Many nursery school activities require that all the children in a class participate at the same time. These interactions give children a chance to play and learn together, but also require them to sit still, listen to stories, and sing songs. If your child isn't used to group activities, you can start introducing them yourself.

Take her to story time at your local library, for instance, or join a moms and tots class to get her used to playing with other children.

Is used to keeping a regular routine

Nursery schools usually follow a predictable routine: ring time, play time, snack, playground, then lunch. There's a good reason for this. Children tend to feel most comfortable and in control when the same things happen at the same time each day. So if your child doesn't keep to a schedule and each day is different from the last, it will help to standardise her days a bit before she starts preschool.

Start by offering meals at regular times. You could also plan to visit the park each afternoon, and stick to a bedtime ritual (bath, then books, and bed).

Has the physical stamina for nursery school

Whether it's a half-day or full-day programme, nursery school keeps children busy. There are art projects to do, field trips to take, and playgrounds to explore. Does your child thrive on activities like this, or does she have trouble moving from one thing to the next without getting cranky?

Another thing to consider is how and when your child needs to nap. Nursery schools usually schedule nap-time after lunch. If your little one still needs a mid-morning snooze, it might not be time yet to go to school. You can work towards building her stamina by making sure she gets a good night's sleep. If you have some flexibility in your schedule, let her attend nursery school for an hour or two to start, gradually increasing the time until she is able to cope with a full morning.

Has language and listening skills

She should be able to use simple three to five word sentences and express her needs and tell you what has happened in the recent past. She should be able to follow simple directions, and listen to a story for several minutes and then talk about it.

Is toilet trained

Your child should be able to tell the teacher when she needs to use the bathroom. She should be able to use the toilet properly, but may still need some help with wiping and will need to be reminded to wash hands and flush.

CHOOSING A NURSERY SCHOOL

If financial and other constraints do not apply, try to visit several possible options to get a good idea of what could suit you and your child before enrolling her. You know your child best and you should trust your feelings.

Questions to ask the principal/owner of the school

- Please show me your registration certificate and inspection reports.
- How long have you and your staff been working with children?
- What are your qualifications? And that of your staff?
- Can I look around the building to see the rooms and outside play area?
- Where will my child rest? What do they rest on?
- Please show me the daily routine charts.
- Are there lots of fun activities to help children learn and play?
- Can children plan some of these themselves?
- How do you encourage good behaviour? What are your discipline methods?
- Will my child be with the same group of children every day, and will they be of a similar age?
- How many children are in a group?
- How will you inform me of my child's progress? Do you have term reports/parent meetings?
- Do the children go on outings and visits?
- How much fundraising is involved in the school – do the fees cover all costs?
- Is there a PTA (parent teacher association)?
- Do parents have plenty of opportunity to say what they want for their children?

Pay attention to the following when you visit

- Check that the hours and term times suit you.
- Are the children calm, safe and happy?
- Do the children play and talk together?
- Are the staff friendly and joining in with what the children are doing?
- Are the staff listening to the children and answering them carefully?
- Are there plenty of clean toys and equipment for children to use?
- Is the school clean, well-kept and safe for children with a fun outside play area?
- Is the playground safely fenced off and are gate openings high up out of a child's reach?
- Do not be afraid to ask questions – good childcare staff expect questions!

EASE THE TRANSITION

If your toddler has never been to playschool, starting nursery school may be the first time that she will be separating from you, so expect her to feel anxious and apprehensive. Try these tips to ease the transition for both of you:

- Trust your instinct – if you don't get a good 'feel' – don't enrol your child if you have other options.
- Visit the school beforehand – take your toddler there a few times beforehand to familiarise her with the new surroundings
- If possible, find a playmate beforehand who attends the same school – it always helps to see a familiar face.
- Teach your toddler some independence beforehand – let her get used to being separated from you for a few hours each day before D day.
- Let her walk, don't carry her in – the wrench at crunch time will be difficult for both of you to handle.
- Distract her as you are arriving and walking in – say, "Wow! Look at that nice swing! Let's go and try it out."
- Don't linger – be firm and encouraging. Tell her that she is safe and loved, then leave.
- Try not to be late in picking her up – it is not fair if all the other kids have gone home and your little one is wondering where you are.
- Be confident and positive – if you are, so will your toddler be.
- Trust the teacher – once you are happy with your decision about your toddler's school and her teacher, allow the teachers to take control whilst your child is in their care.

If your child is still anxious, clingy and cries inconsolably when you leave her at nursery school and after two to three weeks is showing no signs of improvement, consider keeping her at home for a while and trying again later. In some cases, a change of school may be necessary. If the problem persists, consider a psychological assessment.

Extra-mural activities

You may be feeling pressurised to enrol your child in every extra-mural activity on offer. Stimulation in the form of gym, swimming, music, karate, ballet or modern dancing can be most beneficial for your child, but beware of over-scheduling your child. Choose her extra mural activities with care, bearing in mind your child's temperament and personality, as well as being aware of the hazards of over-stimulation.

FLEXIBLE ROUTINE

- Your toddler should be eating from all the food groups spread over three small meals a day, with snacks in between.
- Her milk and calcium intake should be in the region of 500 ml in 24 hours.

- She will be attending playschool or nursery school for most of the morning.
- She will be sleeping once a day, usually after lunch. The sleep will vary from one to three hours in duration.
- She will manage in the region of 6 hours of awake time in the morning before needing a nap.
- If she has dropped her day sleep, bedtime should be at 6 pm. If she is still sleeping in the day, bedtime should be between 6 and 7 pm, depending on what time she woke up in the afternoon.
- She should be sleeping for 11-12 hours at night.
- She should be sleeping for 13–14 hours in a 24 hour cycle.

ACTIVITIES AND TOYS TO ENHANCE DEVELOPMENT

Play is the business of childhood. There is a lot happening out there – overcoming mental and physical challenges, building imagination, skill building and problem solving. Using her ability to pretend, she can transform a garden stone into a cellphone, and a leaf into a boat. Encourage her imagination; it is the cornerstone of her world, and fantasy play opens up a whole new world of creativity. Pretend along with her to show her that you accept her make-believe world, and that something that she is interested in is fun and important to you too.

Outdoor play is crucial for your toddler's ***gross-motor development***. Climbing, swinging, jumping and running will further improve her sense of ***balance and movement***. Encourage her to push and pull heavy objects such as a playmate in a wagon. Helping you dig and rake in the garden will improve her co-ordination. Construction games such as clicking together and building objects, cutting, sticking and drawing will enhance her ***fine-motor skills*** and improve ***hand-eye co-ordination***, as well as begin to teach her some problem solving tasks.

SENSE-ABLE SECRET
Remember that your toddler's favourite toy is you. Well-selected toys will encourage him to play alone, but even the most fascinating toy is much more fun when mom's involved too.

Your toddler is old enough now to have some focused attention on a task. This is when she is able to organise a goal-directed activity whilst remaining calm and still (such as threading a bead onto a piece of string). Teach her how to organise her toys by colour and shape, or biggest to smallest (a box of smarties is ideal for this) – this will help to improve her visual perception skills. As she gets closer to four years of age, play a game by placing three to four familiar objects on a tray. Name them with her, then cover the tray up and encourage her to remember what they were. This is a great memory game.

Try to spend some quiet time with her once a day building a puzzle. To enhance both visual and ***auditory*** perception play "I spy with my little eye". Describe something in a manner that she will understand (gradually introduce more detail in your explanation as she understands more). Let her point to anything that may match the general description.

Singing songs, playing musical instruments and reading stories or listening to story tapes together will improve her listening and ***language*** skills. Action rhymes and songs help to develop a sense of body awareness (for example, "Simple Simon says put your hands on your head ...").

To enhance her ***spatial*** perception, ask her to place objects under tables or behind cushions and ask her to explain to you where you should find them. Tell her where she is in space all the time, for example that she is sitting in a chair which is on the carpet, and that the bike is in front of the door.

Introduce more flavoured and textured food to her diet, and encourage her to ***feel*** it as well as ***taste*** it. Sucking thick liquid (such as yoghurt or custard) through a straw helps develop the muscles of the cheek and jaw to aid speech development. Expose her to many new and interesting ***smells*** (such as paint or bleach).

See table on pages 28–30 for suggestions to calm or stimulate his **sensory system**.

CONTROLLED TV WATCHING

Toddlers are active, interactive and hands-on learners. They need to exercise their minds, muscles and social skills by playing and interacting with other children and adults. Television watching is a passive activity, requiring no response or participation from your child in any way. Remember that toddlers are unable to filter information appropriately, so they cannot tell what is true or false, real or unreal, safe or dangerous. Your toddler runs the risk of sensory overload when watching TV , especially cartoons, or playing computer games. The loud, shrill sounds and very busy, and often violent, visual scenes can hype your toddler into inappropriate behaviour such as aggression, or can cause the opposite effect where she will sit in a trance-like state seemingly 'watching', but in fact she is not benefiting from any stimulation (especially on an auditory level). For these reasons, excessive television watching is not recommended for young children. If your toddler does watch television, make sure that you control her viewing to age-appropriate, toddler specific programmes, or videos. Better still, watch programmes with her so that you can relate them to reality, if necessary.

Ideas for toys and equipment

- outdoor equipment such as a jungle gym, slide and swing.
- black ride-on scooter
- tricycle
- go cart
- plastic wheelbarrow and gardening accessories
- sandpit and accessories
- wendy house
- miniature household apparatus including a broom, mop and ironing board with iron
- plastic tipper trucks
- paddling pool and accessories
- plastic farm animals

- playdough
- dress up and fantasy clothes
- children's scissors, glue and crayons
- blackboard and chalk
- sticker book with stickers
- matching and sorting games
- music tapes or compact discs

These are some simple ideas to play with your child to enhance his development. For more in-depth stimulation ideas, try these books:

- *Clever talk* by Martie Pieterse (Metz Press. 1999)
- *School readiness through play* by Martie Pieterse (Metz Press. 2001)
- *Brain gym for all* by Melodie de Jager (Human & Rousseau. 2001)
- *Entertaining and educating babies and toddlers* by Roby Gee and Susan Meredith (Usborne. 1986)

A LAST WORD

Your toddler's journey as a toddler is now over and the age of pre-school (then big school) is dawning. I leave you with the challenge to find the balance between nurturing, protecting and guiding your child, and allowing her to explore, experiment and become an independent and unique person.

Give her the wings to fly
The heart to love deeply
And the spirit to embrace all the beauty in life.

ANONYMOUS

APPENDIX A

Sensory integration dysfunction (SID)

To the outsider, Andrew (3 years), with his chubby face and sturdy legs, looks like a normal toddler. But his mom, Angela, knows otherwise. Andrew is often irritable, tires easily, and has many emotional outbursts (his mom calls them 'melt downs'. It seemed as though the slightest little thing sets him off, especially in crowded and noisy places. He is terrified of swings and slides, and seems to be thrown off balance by the slightest movement. He struggles to carry heavy objects that his peers manage with ease, and hates to be touched, especially on his head. Needless to say, Angela dreads bath time as normal activities like washing Andrew's hair and brushing his teeth trigger off a storm of tears and tantrums. Andrew hates to be held, so Angela feels frustrated and rejected when she is unable to calm him down easily with a hug. Andrew's behaviour, coupled with the fact that he is a poor sleeper, is taking its toll on Angela's marriage and there are some days when she feels like running away.

As you know by now, sensory integration is the learning process by which accurate information from our senses is interpreted by the brain so that we can respond to our environment in an organised way. A. Jean Ayres (Ph.D), an occupational therapist, was the first person to describe sensory integration as far back as the early 1970s, referring to sensory information as food for the brain. Most of us develop sensory integration automatically, but in some children, this process may go awry. Difficulty in processing and organising sensory information (via our sensory system) may result in short circuits and loss of information in our nervous system. Jean Ayres says, "Good sensory processing enables all the impulses to flow easily and reach their destination quickly. Sensory Integration Dysfunction is a sort of 'traffic jam' in the brain. Some bits of sensory information get 'tied up in traffic', and certain parts of the brain do not get the sensory information they need to do their jobs." (*Sensory Integration and the Child*. Los Angesles Western Psychological Services. 1994.)

UNPLEASANT SENSATIONS

Children suffering from Sensory Integration Dysfunction (SID) may receive inaccurate or unreliable sensory input, so their ability to process information and create appropriate responses is disrupted. They often exhibit a bewildering variety of symptoms – most often thought of as difficult or naughty behaviour. Imagine feeling that every hug or embrace is torture, that every noise sounds like clanging bells, or that the wrinkle in your sock feels like a thousand nails in your foot. For children suffering from Sensory Integration Dysfunction, life is a roller coaster of unpleasant sensations.

Because Andrew spends most of his time trying to protect himself from this seemingly unpredictable world around him, and has difficulty with his motor skills and play activities, it is hard for him to make friends and be part of a group. This could cause him to become a loner, or develop aggressive tendencies to cope with the confusion he is feeling. When Andrew gets over-stimulated, the fine interaction between the sensory system and the brain (sensory modulation) disintegrates and he will have difficulty in controlling his internal thermostat – this is why he is so uncomfortable in crowded and noisy environments.

DEFENSIVE BEHAVIOUR

The more sensitive Andrew is to any form of input, the less he can ***habituate*** to his environment (see page 19). His reaction is called a ***defensive behaviour.*** Children who react with fright to touch will appear to be shy and reluctant to communicate, and may attempt to move away from groups of people (in the fear of being pushed and handled) and will use their body language to make it quite clear that they don't want to be approached. Children who are intolerant or fearful of sounds and noises in the environment are auditory (hearing) defensive. Hypersensitivity to light or avoidance of eye contact may be an indication of visual (sight) defensiveness, and fear or avoidance of certain movements or unstable surfaces show that the child is defensive in the vestibular (movement) area. Daily activities such as car travel, outings to shopping centres or playschool, and hygiene and grooming (combing hair or brushing teeth) can be exhausting and difficult for the whole family.

The problem with any defensive behaviour is that it often causes the child to be 'super-sensitive' to his environment. He is constantly in the active-alert state, and is unable to wind down or switch off. This child may go through a room like a tornado, tipping toys out of the toy box, showing momentary interest in one object, but becoming distracted very quickly before moving on the next object that interests him. However, some children with SID (like Andrew) are so afraid of, and sensitive to their environment, that they are fearful and will not explore.

CAUSES OF SID

So what causes SID? The exact causes are unclear, but in many cases it can be associated with personal life experiences such as prematurity, or it may also be genetic. Angela is afraid of heights and hates loud music.

HE'S NOT NAUGHTY

Children with this disorder are not being naughty. Sensory Integration Dysfunction is not a behavioural disorder, but is due to neurological immaturity, especially of the sensory system.

SYMPTOMS

Because of the complexity of the various areas of the nervous system which are dependent upon and interact with each other (much like a computer) as well as the fact that every child's environment and personality are unique, there is no single list of symptoms which identify Sensory Integration Dysfunction. *This condition affects each child in a different way.* Some children have difficulty with only one sense (such as being auditory defensive which would make them sensitive to loud noises); and some have difficulty with several senses, where they can be either hypersensitive (like Andrew), or have an extremely low level of sensitivity. Children who are under-sensitive simply don't feel things and sensations in their environment strongly enough, so they seek extreme levels of sensation to compensate (like someone who stamps his foot to regain feeling when it has 'gone to sleep'). This makes them appear hyperactive and aggressive.

Some of the signs that may indicate that your child may have Sensory Integration Dysfunction include the following:

- Inability to calm down or unwind.
- Low activity levels – avoids gross motor activities such as running, jumping, climbing and playing and may always be tired and lacking in energy.
- Difficulty making transitions from one activity to another.
- Aversion to being touched, eating foods with certain textures, getting hands messy with finger paint or mud and wearing certain clothing.
- Problems with fine motor skills such as drawing, zipping and dressing; and gross motor skills such as throwing and catching and riding a tricycle.
- Troubled by ordinary sounds, smells and sights. May cover ears when exposed to any noise or avoid eye contact.
- Any delay in language development.
- Poor sleeping patterns, including needing extensive help to fall asleep, for example, being rocked to sleep or driven in a car.
- Craving loud music and touch, and seems oblivious to pain (for example: may continuously throw himself onto the floor or bump his head repeatedly on purpose).
- High activity levels – crashes into things and is continuously swinging, jumping and spinning, and inability to sit and play unattended for a short period of time.
- Dislikes changes in routines or plans, becoming stubborn and controlling.
- Has difficulty focusing in a noisy environment, for example cannot sit still and eat in a busy restaurant.

- Anxious about walking barefoot on grass, sand, cold tiles or rough carpets.
- Becomes upset when his head is tipped back during nappy changes or during bathing.
- Excessive licking, chewing or mouthing of non-food objects.
- Has a very limited repertoire of food choices, gags on lumpy or mixed food textures. Resists tooth brushing or dental work.
- Seeks out vibration excessively, for example audio speakers or washing machine.

If your toddler shows any of the above symptoms, watch him carefully to determine if they are interfering with his physical and emotional development, his ability to play appropriately for his age, and to develop independence. Some of these signs may be an indication of Attention Deficit Disorder, which is a symptom of Sensory Integration Dysfunction. If you are worried, please speak to your healthcare provider who will refer you for an assessment with an occupational therapist who specializes in sensory integration therapy. Alternatively contact the South African Association Sensory Integration (SAISI) which is based at the Occupational Therapy Association (OTASA): Telephone Number: 012-365 1317/1327 or email them at **otoffice@uitweb.co.za**; or look on the SAISI website **www.instsi.co.za** to find a regional liaison contact who can direct you to a qualified SI therapist in your area.

HOW THERAPY CAN HELP

Occupational therapy effectively deals with these issues through a thorough assessment of your child's specific problem areas through observation, standardised test procedures and questionnaires. In the toddler age-group, your child's difficulties may be managed with a home programme or weekly therapy sessions. Both would be individually designed for your child and comprise a variety of exercises and activities to meet his sensory needs in a step by step way. Occupational therapy will increase his comfort zone, and help him through neurological maturation to respond more appropriately to people and situations in his environment.

Autistic spectrum disorder

APPENDIX B

Some children are diagnosed with Autistic Spectrum Disorder in their toddler years. Autistic Spectrum Disorder is a complex neurological condition of which the causes are not clear. It is an umbrella term that includes both high and low-functioning autistic children. In other words, some children may simply be 'a bit odd and grow up to be eccentric adults' but still have full intellectual capacity, while others may be affected more severely to the extent that they are incapable of functioning fully within normal society. The exact cause of the disorder is unknown, but it is believed to be genetic. Common signs of Autistic Spectrum Disorder may include:

- Impairment in the use of ***non-verbal behaviours*** such as eye contact, facial expression, body postures and gestures that determine social interaction.
- Failure to develop relationships with peers (age-appropriate).
- A lack of spontaneous showing, bringing or pointing out of objects of interest.
- A lack of social or emotional responses to others.
- Impairment in normal, age-appropriate communication such as a delay in language development; inability to sustain conversations; stereotyped and repetitive use of language.
- Inability to engage in age-appropriate make-believe or imitative play.
- Restricted, repetitive and stereotyped patterns of behaviour, interests and activities such as obsessive preoccupation with an interest or parts of objects; an inflexible adherence to specific, seemingly unimportant routines, rituals or mannerisms (such as hand or finger flapping, arranging toys in rows, spinning of the body or objects).
- Poor regulation of emotions and sensory input.

(Adapted from: *The Diagnostic Statistical Manual IV.* American Psychiatric Association, Washington, USA, 1994.)

If you are worried about your toddler's development, and he is displaying three or more of the above symptoms, please seek professional help. With early diagnosis and a comprehensive, integrated and developmental relationship-based treatment approach, many children originally diagnosed with ASD are learning to relate to others with warmth, empathy and emotional flexibility.

For support and information, contact Autism SA: 011 486-3696/0834495179, email patsie@iafrica.com or Autism Western Cape: (021) 5573573/5562600.

REACH: Jenny Buckles is the mother of three autistic children. Through her experience and exposure to Applied Behaviour Analysis (ABA), she has set up an organisation which trains therapists in this approach. Contact her on 0835085807 or email info@reach-autism.com.

Two ways to wean

APPENDIX C

COLD TURKEY

This describes the process of replacing all breastfeeds with formula feeds within a period of 24 hours. This usually happens when you have simply had enough, or other circumstances prevail, preventing you from continuing with breastfeeding, for example illness or trauma, or the toxic effects of certain medication. Once your baby has turned a year old, it is likely that you are feeding only once to four times a day, so this method should not be too painful.

If you are breastfeeding more than once a day, I recommend that you ask your pharmacist for medication that inhibits the release of your milk-producing hormones. In addition, anti-inflammatory and pain-relieving medication can be taken orally in tablet form, or rubbed directly onto the breasts in cream form. In some instances, a mild diuretic is prescribed to relieve water retention. Seek your pharmacist's advice. If you are only breastfeeding once a day, you should be able to wean without the need for medication.

Cold cabbage leaves – placed inside your bra and replaced frequently when they start 'cooking' – are a wonderful folk remedy that really works! Wear a firm bra with support, but don't bind your breasts.

If you are in great discomfort, it is acceptable to express a small amount of milk until your breasts feel comfortable (but are not empty and soft). Try not to do this more than twice a day. Discard this milk if you are on medication, but keep it for your toddler if you are not. You may have to do this for about a week, gradually decreasing the frequency and the amount of time spent expressing.

Watch out for signs of mastitis (inflammation of the mammary glands), such as red, lumpy and swollen breasts with associated chills, fever and flu-like symptoms. Massage Arnica cream or an anti-inflammatory cream onto identifiable red, swollen areas, which may be caused by a blocked milk duct and keep cold compresses on the affected breast to reduce swelling. (A small packet of frozen peas is very useful!)

A fairly rare complication of weaning may be the formation of a breast abscess as a result of untreated mastitis. Seek professional medical help. You will need antibiotic medication and, in some cases, drainage of the abscess.

GRADUAL WEANING

This process of weaning usually takes a period of time – generally about two weeks from start to finish.

Begin by replacing one breastfeed a day with a growing-up milk (or full cream cow's milk). The lunchtime feed is usually a good one to start with. Never offer the breast at this time again. If you can, wait until the evening feed is due, and proceed to breastfeed as usual. If you are very uncomfortable, gently rub some Arnica cream onto your breast and place a cold compress or cabbage leaf in your bra. Resist the temptation to express milk but if you simply have to, only express until you are comfortable, not until the breast is empty. Within 48–72 hours the lack of demand for a breastfeed at that specific time will significantly alter the production of milk for that feed and you should no longer experience any discomfort. On day three (not before), or whenever you are ready to drop another feed, proceed as before. This can be either the morning or the evening feed. Three days later drop the last feed. By proceeding slowly, the production of your breast milk will slowly decrease, according to supply and demand, with less risk of breast engorgement, mastitis and abscess formation.

STARTING AGAIN

It is not unusual for toddlers to still be breastfed at least once a day, so don't feel pressurised to wean your toddler off the breast as long as everyone is happy. Weaning may be achieved within 24 hours, or it may take you the next few years. Your individual circumstances and needs will determine exactly how long it will take. If you change your mind about weaning and want to resume breastfeeding, it is very easy to re-lactate. Ask your clinic sister to help you re-establish breastfeeding.

Recipes

APPENDIX D

Use these easy recipes for playdough and bubbles. Your toddler will have hours of fun, especially if you are actively involved in his journey of discovery. Playdough is an excellent medium to develop his sense of touch as well as fine motor-skills. Blowing bubbles is not only great fun, it also develops hand-eye coordination as well as the muscles of the cheek and jaw required for speech.

PLAYDOUGH

500 ml (2 cups) flour
10 ml (2 t) oil
125 ml (½ cup) salt
10 ml (2 t) food colouring of your choice

Mix ingredients together. Add water slowly to make a malleable dough.
Store in a sealed container.

BUBBLES

Combine 50 ml of water with 50 ml dishwashing liquid.

Healthy snacks and food

These recipes are for healthy meals and snacks, all quick and easy to prepare.

BRAN MUFFINS

The uncooked mixture may be refrigerated for up to 2 weeks. Add a cup of raisins, fruit cake mix, chopped nuts or dates for variety.

2 eggs
375 ml (1½ cups) brown sugar
125 ml (½ cup) sunflower oil
500 ml (2 cups) bran
12 ml (2½ t) bicarbonate of soda
625 ml 2½ cups) cake flour
pinch salt
500 ml (2 cups) milk
5 ml (1 t) vanilla essence

Beat together eggs and sugar, then add the oil.
Mix dry ingredients together in another bowl.
Mix milk and vanilla essence, and alternating with the egg mixture, add to the dry ingredients until all the ingredients are thoroughly mixed.
Spoon the mixture into a container, cover and refrigerate overnight.
Bake in muffin pans at 180 °C for 15–20 minutes.

CRUNCHIES

500 ml (2 cups) oats
250 ml (1 cup) sugar
250 ml (1 cup) cake flour
375 ml (1½ cups) butter
500 ml (2 cups) coconut
25 ml (1 T) maple syrup
5 ml (1 t) bicarbonate of soda
pinch of salt

Melt the butter and syrup – set aside.
Mix dry ingredients together.
Add melted butter mix to dry ingredients and stir till well mixed.
Press into a greased baking tray.
Bake at 180 °C for 20 minutes until golden.
Cut into squares while hot.

DATE BALLS

1 egg
250 g butter
500 g soft pitted dates
one packet of Marie biscuits
125 ml (½ cup) sugar
coconut

Heat butter and dates together over low heat and set aside.
Beat egg and sugar together and add to date mix.
Crush biscuits and add to mixture.
Allow mixture to cool.
Shape into small balls and roll in coconut.

QUICHE

Into a greased pie-plate place any chopped cold meat, tuna, sweetcorn or vegetables. Add sliced tomato and/or vegetables and some chopped parsley.
Mix together

250 ml (1 cup) milk
2 eggs
2 heaped tablespoons of wholewheat flour
Salt and pepper

Pour mixture over lined pie-plate. Sprinkle with grated cheese.
Bake at 180 °C for 35 minutes.

PICK 'N MIX MUESLI

Bowl of rolled oats and bran flakes mixed
Bowl of rice crispies and cornflakes mixed
Bowl of sunflower seeds
Bowl of mixed dried fruit, cut up into small pieces
Few pieces of mixed fresh fruit, cut up into small pieces
Yoghurt or milk to serve

Allow your toddler to pick small handfuls of the ingredients in front of her to make up her own breakfast. Store leftovers separately in airtight containers for re-use.

BANANA BREAD

You could substitute mashed banana for veggies

115 g butter
250 ml (1 cup) soft brown sugar
2 eggs beaten
2 bananas mashed, or 1 cup cooked carrots, pumpkin, butternut or baby marrow
240 g flour
10 ml (2 t) baking powder
25 ml (1 T) milk

Cream together the butter and sugar. Add the eggs and mashed fruit/vegetables. Sift in the flour and baking powder. Add the milk and mix well. Pour into a greased loaf pan and bake for 45 minutes at 200 °C.

REFERENCES

References and further reading

A Season for Simplicity. Christian Art Publishers. RSA. 2001

Ayers, A. Jean: *Sensory Integration and the Child.* Los Angesles Western Psychological Services. 1994.

De Gangi, G: *Paediatric disorders of Regulation in Affect and Behaviour – A therapist's guide to Assessment and Treatment.* Academic Press. 2000

DeGangi, G. et al.: *Infant/Toddler Symptom Checklist. A Screening Tool for Parents.* Tuscon, AR: Therapy Skill Builders 1995.

Dunn, W: *Infant/Toddler Sensory Profile: User's Manual.* The Psychological Corporation/Therapy Skills Builders 2002

Eberlein, T: *Sleep: How to teach your child to sleep like a baby.* Pocket Books. New York. 1996.

Edwards, R: *Body Space Integration – Accelerate Pre-school enrichment programmes.* Educational Workshop Cape Town. 1987

Edwards, R: *Visual Perceptual Processing – Accelerate Pre-school enrichment Programmes.* Educational Workshop Cape Town. 1987.

Exley, H: *Wisdom for the Millennium.* Exley. USA/UK. 1999.

Faure, M & Richardson, A: *Baby sense.* Metz Press. 2002

Focus 2001, No 1, page 18-19: *The scourge of worms.*

Green, C: *Toddler Taming Tips, A Parent's Guide to the First Four Years.* Vermillion. London 2003

Greenspan, S and Wieder, S: *The Child with Special Needs: encouraging intellectual and emotional growth.* Perseus Books. 1998.

Greive, B: *Dear Mum.* Robson Books. UK. 2002

Hannaford, C: *Smart Moves.* Great River Books. USA. 1995

Jackson, D: *Parenting With Panache.* Wordsmiths. Johannesburg 2002

Mackenzie S. and Bailey K: *Sensory Diet.* SAISI Newsletter Vol 14 No 3 (2004)

Miller, L: *Assessment of Pre-schoolers* – 1983

Oetter P Frick; S, Richter E; *MORE – Integrating the Mouth with Sensory Functions.* PDP Press USA (2001).

Ohrbach, B: *All Things Are Possible.* Clarkson. N. Potter. New York. 1995.

Pieterse, M: *Clever talk.* Metz Press. RSA. 1999.

Pieterse, M: *School readiness through play.* Metz press. RSA. 2002.

Saturday Star, 4 December 2004: *Lost in a World of Their Own.*

Schaefer, C. and DiGeronimo, T: *Ages & Stages.* Wiley; New York; 2000.

Sensory integration quarterly. Spring 1993, Zoe Mailloux, MA, OTR

Solarsh, B; Katz, B; Green, V; Goodman, M: *START.* University of the Witwatersrand – Sunshine Centre. 1990.

Stock-Kranowitz, C: *The Out of Synch Child.*

Stoppard, M: *You and Your Toddler.* Dorling Kindersley. 2002.

Stoppard, M: *New Baby Care Book* South African Edition. Struik. 1993.

Weissbluth, M: *Healthy sleep habits, happy child.* Ballantine New York. 1999.

Williams, MS and Shellenberger, S: *How does your Engine Run – A leader's guide to the Alert programme for self-regulation.* Therapy Works, USA (1996).

Your Baby Magazine, August 2004: Article: *Choose Your Words*

Your Baby Magazine, December 2004: Article: *Choosing appropriate toys.*

INDEX